HOW TO
BE GOOD
WITHOUT
REALLY
TRYING

HOW TO
BE GOOD
WITHOUT
REALLY
TRYING

LETTING JESUS LIVE HIS LIFE IN YOU

Mike Flynn

Chosen

Grand Rapids, Michigan

© 2004 by Mike Flynn

Published by Chosen Books
A division of Baker Book House Company
P.O. Box 6287, Grand Rapids, MI 49516-6287
http://www.bakerbooks.com

Printed in the United States of America

Library of Congress Cataloging-in-Publication Data
Flynn, Mike, 1940-
    How to be good without really trying : letting Jesus live his life in you / Mike Flynn.
        p.   cm.
    Includes bibliographical references.
    ISBN 0-8007-9357-9 (pbk.)
    1. Christian life. I. Title.
BV4501.3.F59 2004
248.4—dc22   2003024168

Contents

Acknowledgments

The author wishes to thank these friends who have lent their very helpful discernment and wisdom in the critique of this book: Donna Bowker, my wife, Sue Flynn, Dan Smith and Jan Thornton.

Special thanks to Jane Campbell and Grace Sarber for their excellent professional collaboration.

In my first book, *Holy Vulnerability*, I quoted S. D. Gordon: "You can do more than pray *after* you have prayed, but you cannot do more than pray *until* you have prayed. . . . Prayer is striking the winning blow; service is gathering up the spoils." There are many who strike the winning blow for me. It is my very great pleasure and honor, therefore, to dedicate this book to those who regularly intercede for FreshWind Ministries and me. Spread throughout several denominations, they all conduct wonderful ministries.

These precious prayer warriors are: Larry and Pat, Robert, Allyn and Joan, Joanne, Pam, Sonia, Cliff and Geraldine, Tom, Betty, Peter and Audrey, Rev. Bill and Bev, Bob and Donna, John, Mary, Barb, Jack and Lu, Jean, Donald, Ted, Jane, Shirley, Carole, Pat, Bobby, Bob, Rev. David and Ginny, Maggie, Clarence and Ann, Ann, John, Linda, Ron, David, Bert, Harry and

ACKNOWLEDGMENTS

Norma, Mac and Barb, Mary, Lori, Marilyn, David and Tricia, Jason and Laura, Kevin, Joel, Rosemary, Roy and Ann, Leon and Rhea, Linda, Jan, Bp. Sandy and Gigi, Rev. Doug and Catherine, Gary and Catherine, Ben and Marty, John and Catherine, Diana, John, Steve and Cathy, Brewster and Pam, Cathleen, Don and Kay, June, Revs. Kent and Geri, Lloyd and Carol Ann, Sally, Gail, Gale, Sandy, Ray, Dick and Kay, Marolyn, Carolyn, Sally, Vee, Dora, June, Rev. Chuck and Jan, Rev. Kit and Kathy, Rev. John and Laurie, Edwin, Becky, Anne Marie, Edi, Sheila, Rev. John, Chris and Carol, Bonnie, Donna, Joy, Rev. Ken and Ginger, TR, Rev. Kevin, Ruby, Ginny, Sharon, Ann, Barb, Robert and Gail, Susan, Dave and Audrey, Beth, Dan, Douglass, Rev. Lenny, Neil and Margie, Dr. Carl and Pat, Durwood and Laurie, Rev. Rand and Kathryn, Richard and Eileen, Rev. Joe and Tina, Sharon, Geri, Bill and Susalee, Diane, Jon and Pat, Teresa, Ethel, Jack and Doris, Rev. Chuck and Ruthanne, Rev. Vic and Leanne, Ben, John and Diane, Sharon, Bill and Bonnie, Mary, Edwina, Bob and Diane, Lou and Pat, Rev. John, Elizabeth, John and Lori, Gary and Cyndee, Cindy, Ron and Dana, Carol, Dr. Nelson and Jean, Brad, Paul and Suzanne, Richard and Brenda.

1

The Commands of Christ

Awaking at my normal time of 5:30 A.M., I got out of bed, put on my bathrobe and quietly closed the door so I would not wake my wife, Sue. I went into the kitchen to grind the strongest coffee beans that Starbucks makes then went outside to get the morning newspaper. I read the paper and sipped coffee until I was fully awake. Then I picked up my Bible and tossed up a quick prayer as I looked for my place: "O Lord, help me understand what You want me to get out of Your Book this morning."

The first chapter I was scheduled to read was 1 Chronicles 29. I remembered from the previous day that King David had declared he would not be permitted to build the Temple but his son Solomon would. I began reading verse 1: "Then King David said to the whole assembly: 'My son Solomon, the one whom God has chosen, is young and inexperienced. The task is great, because this palatial structure is not for man but for the LORD God.'" All of a sudden the Lord said to me, *Resign from your position,* and I had the impression that someone else was to take my church to its next level.

I gulped, and I bet my eyes were wide open.

Next thought: *Go and do conferences full-time.*

I gulped again. Eyes even wider.

For a second I wanted to say, like Bill Cosby's Noah from a skit many years ago, "Who is this really?" But I was fairly convinced that it was the Lord. I will share in chapter 2 how we verify that what we hear is from God. For the moment, I ask you to assume that this was the real deal.

It turned out that this was the culmination of an eight-month process of guidance through which the Lord had been leading me. At that moment, however, the command to resign looked quite daunting. Where would I go? How would I make a living? How would I organize such a thing? When? Why? And at that moment, none of the answers to those questions came.

So I resigned from the church I had pastored for thirteen years. But I had nowhere to go and nothing to do, so the congregation made me the interim pastor. Over the next year the pieces fell into place. Through a series of nudges from God, we moved to Denver and launched FreshWind Ministries on a full-time basis. Since then, we have had a ball leading more than two hundred conferences, seeing God move in wonderful ways and working with thousands of His people. How glad I am that I obeyed His command to resign, even though it was scary at the time!

The Importance of Obeying Jesus

Obeying Jesus frees Him to bless us in ways that would be impossible otherwise. I want you to know those marvelous blessings. For that reason, I have written this book. It centers on the commands and graces of Christ. Its purpose is twofold: first, to let Jesus' orders percolate deep into our souls so that we are inclined to take them radically seriously; and second, to discover the wonderful abilities the Lord makes available to us as we seek to follow His orders.

Why is it important to obey Jesus? In Luke's gospel, Jesus asks an abrupt question: "Why do you call me, 'Lord, Lord,' and do not *do* what I say?" (Luke 6:46). He equates the obedient with those who build on rock and the disobedient with those who build on sand. He makes the same point in Matthew when He talks of wise and foolish builders: "Not everyone who says to me, 'Lord, Lord,' will enter the kingdom of heaven, but only he who *does* the will of my Father who is in heaven" (Matthew 7:21). To obey Him is to be founded on stable rock; to disobey Him is to be founded on shifting sand.

Later in Matthew when He is talking about the final judgment, He sets forth the parable of the wise and foolish virgins, concluding that the Lord will say to the foolish, "I tell you the truth, I don't know you" (Matthew 25:12). He gives a similar answer to people who claimed they had eaten and drunk with Him and had been taught by Him in their streets: "I don't know you or where you come from. Away from me, all you evildoers!" (Luke 13:27). Another of Jesus' rebukes was leveled at the Pharisees and it, too, centered on this matter of commands: "You have let go of the *commands* of God and are holding on to the traditions of men" (Mark 7:8).

On the surface of it, for our own present and eternal well-being, it is important to know what He has told us to do and then to *do* it, by His help. Knowing His commands but not doing them is perilous. Not knowing them is even more perilous. What He is looking for is compliance with His directions.

What Are His Commands?

What has Jesus told us to do? This book attempts to answer that question, as well as to show the means by which we rise to obey Him. I want you to enjoy the fullness of life in Christ while you are yet on this earth, and when your time here is over I want you to enjoy the unimaginable wonders of heaven.

In the gospels Jesus gives us scores of commands:

Repent.

Follow Me.

(Be) poor in spirit, meek, merciful, pure in heart, peacemakers.

Rejoice when persecuted.

Be salt.

Let your light shine.

Do and teach the commandments.

Do not be angry with your brother.

Be reconciled to your brother.

Agree with your adversaries.

Do not look with lust on a woman.

Pluck out the offensive eye.

Swear not at all.

Resist not evil but turn the cheek.

Give your cloak to the one who takes your coat.

Go the second mile.

Lend to a borrower.

Bless those who curse you.

Do good to those who hate you.

Pray for those who despitefully use you.

Be perfect.

Give your alms in secret.

Say the Lord's Prayer.

Lay up treasure in heaven.

Have a single eye.

Serve one master.

Take no thought for your life.

Seek the Kingdom of God and His righteousness.

Judge not.

Cast the beam out of your own eye.

Ask, seek, knock.

Do unto others as you would have them do unto you.

Know others by their fruits.

Do the Father's will.

Learn what it means that God will have mercy and not sacrifice.

Pray for God to send laborers into the harvest.

Go and preach . . . heal . . . cast out . . . cleanse . . . raise the dead.

Be wise as serpents and harmless as doves.

Beware of men.

Do not worry about what to say.

Fear not.

Speak what I tell you.

Fear God.

Confess Me before men.

Deny yourself, take up your cross and follow Me.

Lose your life for My sake.

Be not offended in Me.

Come unto Me.

Take My yoke upon you.

Learn of Me.

Do not blaspheme the Holy Spirit.

Have a good heart.

Be wheat.

Sell all to buy the Kingdom.

Give them something to eat.

Bring them to Me.

Be not afraid.

Do not doubt.

And that list comprises only His commands through the first half of Matthew! There are three-and-a-half more gospels to go, not to mention His commands in the rest of the New Testament!

In an attempt to weigh out these commands, I studied them. First, I simply counted how many times He gave each command. Second, I looked into the Greek to detect when Jesus was giving a command by the imperative form of the verbs He used. Imperatives are commands. They mean, "Take action on this!" Third, I grouped similar commands together in order to make the list more manageable. This book, therefore, examines just seven commands of Jesus, but those seven contain a considerable majority of all His commands.

The top seven commands are: Love, Believe, Forgive, Watch, Give, Grow Up and Hear. In addition, of course, are those commands the Lord gives that are unique to each of us, such as His command to me to resign from my pastorate.

Why This Title?

Why have I chosen to title this book *How to Be Good without Really Trying*? When I was praying and preparing talks for a large conference in Colorado a few years ago, the Lord asked me, *What good am I if I am not good in you?* That question rocked me to the foundation of my being.

At first I wanted to dodge the question: "O Lord, don't make people look to me to see what You are like!" But that was exactly what He meant them to do. I soon realized that He wanted to address that question to every one of His followers. So I asked myself and the people at the conference: What good is Jesus if He is not good in you?

14

Anyone the least bit familiar with the Bible knows that Jesus' worth is unassailable. He was born of a virgin so as not to be tainted with the sin of mankind, which is inherited—in Hebrew thought—through one's father. He maintained His purity and so remained qualified to be nailed to the cross as the sacrifice for the sin of all mankind. He was raised from the dead in order to triumph over all those sins and to offer life to His followers on earth and eternal life to those who persevere.

But it is also clear in the Scriptures that His followers represent Him to the world. "If you hold to my teaching, you really are my disciples" (John 8:31). His followers represent Him either poorly or well.

That night, the worship leader, Kelly Smith, pondered this question and produced a song that everyone sang the next day.

What good is Jesus unless He's good in you?
What good is Jesus unless He's good in you?
Is He faith? No, unless He's faith in you.
Is He joy? No, unless He's joy in you.
Is He peace? No, unless He's peace in you.
Is He love? No, unless He's love in you.

What good is Jesus unless He's good in me?
What good is Jesus unless He's good in me?
Is He mercy? No, unless He's mercy in me.
Is He patience? No, unless He's patience in me.
Is He kindness? No, unless He's kindness in me.
Is He Healer? No, unless He's Healer in me.

What good is Jesus unless He's good in us?
What good is Jesus unless He's good in us?
Is He Savior? Yes! When we ask Him in our hearts.
Is He Lord? Yes, He's Lord of all the earth.
Is He God? Yes, and evermore shall be!
But what good is Jesus unless He's "yes" in me?[1]

This was Kelly's way of putting into her own words what Christianity is all about. It reminds me of what St. John said when he was summarizing Christianity: "Dear friends, if our hearts do not condemn us, we have confidence before God and receive from him anything we ask, because we *obey his commands* and do what pleases him. And this is his *command*: to believe in the name of his Son, Jesus Christ, and to love one another as he *commanded* us. Those who *obey his commands* live in him, and he in them" (1 John 3:21–24). Obeying God gives us confidence and keeps our hearts (our consciences) from condemning us because, at the core, Jesus and we are inseparably blended.

For a time, in fact, I thought the title should be *What Good Is Jesus If He's Not Good in You?* But then, as the book unfolded, it became clear that the Lord was leading me to expound a profound mystery: We are commanded to be good, but only Jesus in us is capable of producing that good in its fullness. There comes a stage of collaboration with God (as later chapters will disclose) in which we easily turn over to Jesus the task of producing good. The subtitle of this book, of course, is the key: *Letting Jesus Live His Life in You.* That is what enables us to be good without really trying.

Meanwhile, let's look at the results of failure to let Him be good in us.

Judgment for Unbelievers

It is clear in the teachings of Jesus that unbelievers will be judged. John the Baptist predicted this: "His winnowing fork is in his hand, and he will clear his threshing floor, gathering his wheat into the barn and burning up the chaff with unquenchable fire" (Matthew 3:12). Jesus told of a future division between mankind: "I say to you that many will come from the east and the west, and will take their places at the feast with Abraham, Isaac and Jacob in the kingdom of heaven. But the subjects of the kingdom will be thrown outside, into the darkness, where there will be weeping and gnashing of teeth" (Matthew 8:11–12). He repeats a similar thought in chapter 13, verses 40–43:

> As the weeds are pulled up and burned in the fire, so it will be at the end of the age. The Son of Man will send out his angels, and they will weed out of his kingdom everything that causes sin and all who do evil. They will throw them into the fiery furnace, where there will be weeping and gnashing of teeth. Then the righteous will shine like the sun in the kingdom of their Father. He who has ears, let him hear.

After teaching about the sheep and the goats, Jesus claimed, "Then they will go away to eternal punishment, but the righteous to eternal life" (Matthew 25:46). And John's gospel comments, "Whoever believes in the Son has eternal life, but whoever rejects the Son will not see life, for God's wrath remains on him" (John 3:36).

Pretend believers come under special condemnation. In Matthew 23 Jesus pronounced a series of woes on Pharisees, the leaders of the religion. Jesus blasted them for hypocrisy, spiritual blindness, misplaced priorities, legalism, greed, self-indulgence, wickedness and the persecution of God's messengers. In Luke He summarizes, "They devour widows' houses and for a show make lengthy prayers. Such men will be punished most severely" (Luke 20:47). Paul logs in on this topic as well: "He will punish those who do not know God and do not *obey* the gospel of our Lord Jesus" (2 Thessalonians 1:8). So the teachings of Jesus clearly declare that those who do not believe in Him will face judgment.

Reward and Punishment for Believers

There are consequences to obeying the Lord. Primary among them is the idea of reward:

> If any man builds on this foundation using gold, silver, costly stones, wood, hay or straw, his work will be shown for what it is, because the Day will bring it to light. It will be revealed with fire, and the fire will test the quality of each man's work. If what he has built survives, he will receive his reward. If it is burned up, he will suffer loss; he himself will be saved, but only as one escaping through the flames.

1 Corinthians 3:12–15

So it is clear that testing will come by fire, and the fire will determine if our work survives—gold, silver, costly stones—or if it is destroyed—wood, hay or straw.

It is important to grasp what this passage is saying. We will be saved, but our work may not. And if our work is burned up, we will suffer loss—even in heaven. Revelation 22:12 confirms this thought: "Behold, I am coming soon! My *reward* is with me, and I will give to everyone according to what he has done."

The basic consequence of obeying Him is reward, while that of disobeying Him is punishment. Second Corinthians 5:10 asserts, "For we must all appear before the judgment seat of Christ, that each one may receive what is due him for the things done while in the body, whether good or bad." It is important that we see the words *all, judgment seat* and *each one*. This is not something that only a few will experience. Everyone will face the Judge. And punishment is a real possibility.

These are not a few lesser-known passages taken out of context. Colossians 3:23–25 reminds us: "Whatever you do, work at it with all your heart, as working for the Lord, not for men, since you know that you will receive an inheritance from the Lord as a *reward*. It is the Lord Christ you are serving. Anyone who does wrong will be repaid for his wrong, and there is no favoritism." Jesus confirms this in Matthew 16:27: "For the Son of Man is going to come in his Father's glory with his angels, and then he will *reward* each person according to what he has done."

Toward the end of His public ministry, Jesus told a parable whose point was fruitfulness: "'Sir,' the man replied, 'leave it alone for one more year, and I'll dig around it and fertilize it. If it bears fruit next year, fine! If not, then cut it down'" (Luke 13:8–9).

Just a few verses earlier, Jesus concluded another parable: "That servant who knows his master's will and does not get ready or does not do what his master wants will be beaten with many blows. But the one who does not know and does things deserving punishment will be beaten with few blows" (Luke 12:47–48).

Jesus told 38 parables. Six of them had a conclusion that excluded people, eight of them that included people and eighteen that included or excluded people depending upon their behavior. Only five of Jesus' parables did not deal with the matter of inclusivity-exclusivity.

Hebrews 10:26–31 contains three warnings to the believer:

If we deliberately keep on sinning after we have received the knowledge of the truth, no sacrifice for sins is left, but only a fearful expectation of judgment and of raging fire that will consume the enemies of God. Anyone who rejected the law of Moses died without mercy on the testimony of two or three witnesses. How much more severely do you think a man deserves to be punished who has trampled the Son of God under foot, who has treated as an unholy thing the blood of the covenant that sanctified him, and who has insulted the Spirit of grace? For we know him who said, "It is mine to avenge; I will repay," and again, "The Lord will judge his people." It is a dreadful thing to fall into the hands of the living God.

All of these Scriptures point to one inescapable fact: We must grapple with Jesus' expectation that He will judge each of us according to our works.

What about Salvation?

"Well, wait just a minute!" you might exclaim. "What about all these sermons I have heard about grace being free and that we are justified by faith and not by works? I thought heaven was a gift." It is true that salvation, redemption, regeneration, eternal life—whatever term you wish to use—is freely given to us as we have faith in the merits of the death and resurrection of Jesus Christ. No one earns his or her way into heaven. The idea of earning such favor with God was, in fact, one of the heresies in the early Church. It is important, however, that we read everything the Bible says about a given subject, throw out nothing, ask the Spirit for enlightenment and come up with a full and balanced statement of God's position on a given subject.

St. Paul clearly states, "For we maintain that a man is justified by faith apart from observing the law" (Romans 3:28). James equally clearly states, "What good is it, my brothers, if a man claims to have faith but has no deeds? Can such faith save him?" A few verses later he concludes, "Faith by itself, if it is not accompanied by action, is dead" (James 2:14, 17). These two brothers are not in conflict. Paul is approaching the subject of salvation from the pre-entry point; James is looking at it from the post-entry perspective. Paul is saying that you must receive salvation as a gift appropriated by faith; James is saying that if you have truly been saved it will surely show up in your works.

Forgiveness does not mean that judgment is turned aside. "Those whom I love I rebuke and discipline," the Savior says in Revelation 3:19. Hebrews 12, in fact, notes that if believers are not disciplined then they are not real children of God but illegitimate (verse 8). If one responds well to God's discipline, he can be expected to enjoy "a harvest of righteousness and peace" in this life and in the next (verse 11).

Taking into consideration the above-mentioned verses, one might conclude with something like this:

You get *into* heaven by faith;
where you end up in heaven is by works.

If judgment by fire will surely come and there will be reward or punishment awaiting the results of judgment, then some among the saved will be better off than others. I am not talking here about judgment between believers and unbelievers, such as the scene mentioned by Jesus in Matthew 25 in which some "will go away to eternal punishment, but the righteous to eternal life" (verse 46). What I am talking about is judgment for all who have professed faith in Jesus as Savior and Lord.

In summary, there are two kinds of final judgment:

1. Between the saved and the unsaved. The Judge will say to the saved, "You have sinned, but I have paid off your sins. You may enter eternal life." To the unsaved He will say, "Your sins will be paid off by you yourself. Go to the place of eternal punishment."
2. Between the obedient saved and the disobedient saved. To the obedient He will say, "Go to the place of your reward. You have been faithful over a little. So rule ten cities." To the disobedient saved, He will say, "Your failure to obey My commands mandates that you experience punishment to the degree that you disobeyed."

Where, exactly, do the rewarded end up and where do the punished end up? Both will be in heaven, but it is clear that there are differentiations of what it means to be in heaven. Beyond that, we cannot say. Paul mentions "the third heaven" (2 Corinthians 12:2) and "places" (plural) in heaven (Ephesians 1:3, 20; 2:6; 3:10; 6:12); other New Testament writers talk of "heavens" (plural). At best we can say that there are levels or intensities of both reward and punishment in the next life.

Why is this important? Let me do a little math for you. Since eternity is endless, we cannot get our brains around it. So, for purposes of discussion, let's just conceive of eternity as one million years long. On that count, if you live to be 80, eternity will be 12,500 times longer than your life on earth. One of something does not balance out 12,500 of that thing, does it? The point is that you are going to spend the vast majority of your existence *there* rather than here. This life is like an entryway. The whole point of an entryway is to get through it to the larger room where all the action is. You must give considerable thought to your status in eternity.

Obedience

One of the most forthright writers in the Bible is James. If you want to know where you sit with God and man, just read James from start to finish and you will have a pretty good idea. In the first chapter, James makes this clear statement: "Do not merely listen to the word, and so deceive yourselves. *Do* what it says" (verse 22). This brings us back to Jesus' question: "Why do you call me, 'Lord, Lord,' and do not do what I say?" (Luke 6:46).

The operative word is *do*. It is not what you know or believe or understand or articulate that makes points with Jesus. It is what you *do*. One does not *have* faith; one *does* it. I mean that quite straightforwardly. In the Bible, faith is an action verb, not some mystical possession. You possess faith only in the act of doing it.

One straight shooter—like James—was the nineteenth-century novelist George MacDonald. He said this: "Instead of asking yourself whether you believe or not, ask yourself if you have this day done one single thing because He said, 'Do it,' or once abstained because He said, 'Do not do it.' It is simply absurd to say you believe, or even want to believe in Him, if you do not do anything He tells you."[2] First John 2:3–4 echoes this: "We know that we have come to know him if we *obey* his commands. The man who says, 'I know him,' but does not do what he commands is a liar, and the truth is not in him."

Obedience is the true mark of faith and of "followership." When I obey Jesus, I am demonstrating that He is my Lord; when I do not, I am not. Does this end all questions about the subject? Of course not. Whole books have been written about faith. I wrote one myself: *The Mustard Seed Book.* My point in that book was that obedience is an act of will. By founding one's faith in the will rather than in the intellect or emotions, one can exercise sufficient faith as a decisive act. That act frees God to do two things that bring harmony to that act. First, obedience frees understanding. When we obey, we end up understanding why God told us to do something. Second, feelings follow faith. Our obedience frees God to heal or touch our emotions so that they end up agreeing with the act of faith. It took much of *The Mustard Seed Book* to expound and illustrate those points.[3] God gives us freedom from rational confusion and emotional disunity after we take the step of acting in obedience on something that He has told us to do. So obedience is not only crucial to the status of our faith, but it is also the means by which we free God to bless us in unforeseen ways.

"Blessed rather are those who hear the word of God and *obey* it," Jesus said in Luke 11:28. Blessed how? By being regarded as His friends, even as His family: "Whoever does God's will is my brother and sister and mother" (Mark 3:35). I have walked with Him for thirty years now and can testify that there is no greater blessing than being His brother. Some illustrations of that relationship will appear as this book goes along. Often I have had the joy of doing what He told me and seeing the results, like the blind fellow in John 9 who had to obey Jesus' directions to go wash in the pool of Siloam before he experienced the blessing of sight. The order is: Obedience first, then blessings follow.

When the tax collector Zacchaeus declared that he would give half of his wealth to the poor and a fourfold payback to any he had cheated, Jesus said this was evidence of salvation. Zacchaeus had not yet said anything about his beliefs, but he proved them by his actions.

Ruth Ruibal in Cali, Colombia, states, "Obedience always brings life and disobedience always brings death. . . . Unbelief and disobedience are one and the same; so are faith and obedience."[4] This is straightforward talk. The bottom line of faith is action in obedience to Jesus.

We Are the Gospel

We are *not* the Gospel, of course. None of us has ever saved anyone. None of us could qualify to be nailed up on a cross, identified with the sins of even one man, and pay those sins off through our suffering. Only the sinless Son of God can be eligible as a sacrifice for sin, and we are not He. This is why Jesus could utter, "No one comes to the Father except by me." He Himself alone is the bridge across the chasm that a person's sins create between him and the Father. Only Jesus *could* suffer for sin's redemption. Only Jesus *did* suffer for sin's redemption. Only Jesus offers His sacrifice to any and all who will make the decision to believe in and receive His forgiveness and Himself into their hearts. As a bumper sticker put it: "No Jesus, no peace; know Jesus, know peace." The sinner has been called the Gospel's reason for existence. Jesus said, "I have not come to call the righteous, but sinners" (Mark 2:17). But He expects us to answer His call.

After we respond to His call, then Jesus' question eventually becomes unavoidable: "What good am I if I'm not good in you?" He is not referring to His goodness in and of Himself; He is getting at another matter. Jesus has not been seen in His own physical body for nearly two thousand years. If people want to see Jesus, they have to find Him inside you, His follower. To see His face, they will have to look at yours. To hear His voice, they will have to listen to yours.

In Romans 2:24, St. Paul declares, "God's name is blasphemed among the Gentiles because of you." He also claims, "God 'will give to each person according to what he has done'"

(Romans 2:6). What if someone steadfastly refuses to believe in Jesus because of you? A contemporary version of this came through an unbeliever: "Jesus is mean-spirited, selfish and petty, for that is what I see in you Christians."

Why is it important to look for Jesus in the lives of His followers? Because Christianity is not just Jesus and is not just you. It is both. Christianity is *both* Jesus and His followers, the treasure in the earthen vessels. "Christ in you, the hope of glory" (Colossians 1:27) is another way to say it. Not just Christ, not just you, but Christ in you. And again: "Instead, put on the Lord Jesus Christ, and make no provision for the flesh, to gratify its desires" (Romans 13:14, NRSV). C. S. Lewis addressed this: "Putting on Christ . . . is not one among many jobs a Christian has to do; and it is not a sort of special exercise for the top class. It is the whole of Christianity. Christianity offers nothing else at all."[5] In this sense, we are the Gospel—Jesus and us.

This is both the scandal and the glory of Christianity. We disclose Him poorly or well, but there is no one else to disclose Him. To the eyes of the onlooking world, you and I individually and we collectively are the proof or denial of who He says He is.

Look at the words of this prayer by St. Theresa:

Christ has no body now but yours,
No hands, no feet on earth but yours.
Yours are the eyes through which he looks compassion on this
   world.
Yours are the feet with which he walks to do good.
Yours are the hands with which he blesses all the world.
Yours are the hands—Yours are the feet
Yours are the eyes—You are his Body
Christ has no body now but yours,
No hands, no feet on earth but yours.
Yours are the eyes through which he looks compassion on this
   world.
Christ has no body now on earth, but yours.

I do not know how He got up the guts to do it, but Jesus decided that He would put an intermediary between Himself and those who do not know Him, and that intermediary is called the Church. I am not speaking of the Church as an institution or organization or building, but in the way the Book describes it: the Body of Christ. You and me.

Operationally speaking, it is as though the slogan could be reworded like this: "No Body, no Jesus; know Body, know Jesus." Somehow Jesus got up the courage to work this way. Why? Here is the short answer: We humans are made in the image of God. God is Personhood *par excellence*. We humans are persons. When we meet Personhood in the Person of Jesus, our personhood begins to be cleansed, released, empowered and perfected. God thinks that in our personhood we have the potential to disclose Him better than anything else. So I say: Know Body, know Jesus.

What Do They See in Me?

Now let me ask you, if you are a believer, what is your reaction to this? I want you to ask yourself, "What kind of Jesus are people seeing in me?"

Is Jesus critical of people? If I am critical of people, they have every right to conclude that this Jesus whom I represent is critical. Is Jesus sinful? Of course not. But if I am sinful, they have every right to conclude that this Jesus whom I represent is sinful. Don't they? Why not?

How do we land on the criteria for deciding whether or not we are adequately representing Him? Look at what is called the Great Commission: "All authority in heaven and on earth has been given to me. Therefore go and make disciples of all nations, baptizing them in the name of the Father and of the Son and of the Holy Spirit, and teaching them to obey everything I have commanded you. And surely I am with you always, to the very end of the age" (Matthew 28:18–20). This commission or charge is given to every single believer. Jesus places in our hands the need and opportunity to disclose Him to others. What are we to teach them? "Go and make disciples . . . teaching them to *obey* everything I have commanded you."

Here we have the key again. Obeying Jesus is what reveals Him to others. My obedience is the proof to the onlooker that this Jesus stuff works. We can play with the slogan again: "No obedience, no proof; know obedience, know proof."

In the next chapter we will begin to look closely at how you find the ability to discern what He wants you to do at a particular moment and how to obey His commands. But for the present, let the question stand as it is. How well are you displaying Jesus to your world? How accurate a picture of Him do they get from examining you? What do they know about faith, hope and love from looking at you? How much do you *want* to disclose Jesus to others?

Do not immediately beat your breast lamenting what a poor witness you have been. That is not what I am after. Obedience, as I have said, is the sign that one is a believer, a follower of Jesus. Whenever you do something because He told you, you are His follower. Whenever you do not, you are not. He said it clearly: "If you love me, you will *obey what I command*," and "You are my friends if you *do what I command*" (John 14:15; 15:14).

Do you generally conduct yourself with honesty? If so, you are being a follower of Jesus. Do you generally act with compassion toward others? Do you seek to be generous? Do you try to love others? Do you act with forgiveness toward them? Are you trying to believe? Then you are a friend of Jesus.

The crunch comes when He says to do something you do not want to do or that is difficult. But that crunch is also your growing edge. Jesus carefully tailors challenges to fit exactly where we are in life. He is not being cruel. He knows that with His help we can do the things He challenges us to do. Better yet, He knows that if we do those things, we will benefit first, not to mention what our obedience may do for others. He loves us, after all, and is seeking our well-being.

He is wonderfully patient with our failures at crunch time. If I fail, He just punts and looks for another opportunity to organize another crunch by putting a command to me. The more I obey, the more whole I become and the more completely Jesus is displayed in me.

God's Method Is You

Another way to say all this is that God's method is you, and your method is God. God has always insisted on what theologians call incarnality. Incarnality is in-fleshment; it is the spiritual becoming physical. Jesus Christ, of course, was incarnation in fullness. He was the perfect, complete, total incarnation of God in this world. But that does not mean He was a stick figure. C. S. Lewis states:

> God could, had He pleased, have been incarnate in a man of iron nerves, the stoic sort who lets no sigh escape him. Of His great humility He chose to be incarnate in a man of delicate sensibilities who wept at the grave of Lazarus and sweated blood in Gethsemane. Otherwise we should have missed the great lesson that it is by His will alone that a man is good or bad, and feelings are not, in themselves, of any importance. We should also have missed the all-important help of knowing that HE has faced all that the weakest of us face, has shared not only the strength of our nature but every weakness of it but sin. If He had been incarnate in a man of immense natural courage, that would have been for many of us almost the same as His not being incarnate at all.[6]

What Jesus is doing now, of course, is looking for people through whom to reveal Himself—or incarnate Himself—today. While organizations look for better methods, God is always looking for better people. People are God's method. God is continually investing Himself in people so that they can reveal Him to the world.

A friend is fond of saying, "God loves you just as you are—and He loves you too much to leave you the way you are." It is because of His love that the Lord lays these commands upon us.

In the next seven chapters we are going to look at the commands of Christ. On the front end they can look daunting, difficult and even disturbing. But I will share with you several means that God Himself provides once we make up our will that we are going to do what He says. He never asks what He does not enable. Along the way, I will tell you stories of those who have put their faith into action and what the results of their obedience have been. I have pastored thousands of people for more than thirty years and have led more than 350 conferences around the world. I draw on my and others' experiences in order to provide examples of real people in real situations who found grace to obey Jesus' commands.

What follows may be strong meat for you. It is meant to be chewed on, pondered, argued with and digested. Bless you.

The order of the commands is going to be treated in reverse: We will look first at command number 7, then number 6 and so on. This is because you cannot obey what you have not heard. In addition, some of the chapter subtitles reflect what I think are Jesus' thoughts as He issues commands to us and helps us obey them. So we will look first at how to hear God.

2

The Seventh Command: *Hear*

"Learn to Hear Like Me"

When I was 31 years old, the Lord graciously arranged for me to meet Jesus and be empowered by the Holy Spirit. Since I had been a pastor for six years, it was about time! Later, I will tell you more about how it happened. For the moment I want you to know that I soon came to an important realization: Though I had a good education, a fairly competent mind and a relatively healthy emotional life, I was incompetent by myself to decide what I should do. I was not a particularly humble person, but somehow I knew I needed God's input in every decision, every turning point, every opportunity and every problem.

So I began devouring books about getting along with God. I do not remember which particular book this came from, but one helpful assertion stuck with me: "The one thing a servant has a right to is orders." That made sense. If I am trying to serve the King of kings, I need to know what He wants me to do. At first, I thought He might be reluctant to talk to me. I began tossing that thought into God's face. "Aha! Your own Son said, 'Without Me you can do nothing,' so You have got to help me. You must tell me what to do, and You must enable me to do it." My experience—thirty years later—is that God likes that kind of talk. He likes being given the opportunity to speak to us. He even likes when we get lippy about our need for His input.

Jesus' key parable in all three synoptic gospels is the parable of the sower. Why is it the key? First, He teaches about three inappropriate ways of hearing the Word of God: not receiving it, having no root for it and letting life's worries choke the seed of the Word. Then Jesus tells us the one appropriate way: "Others, like seed sown on good soil, hear the word, accept it, and produce a crop—thirty, sixty or even a hundred times what was sown" (Mark 4:20). Hearing and accepting the Word is what allows it to produce a 3,000 percent or 6,000 percent or 10,000 percent return. Before interpreting the parable for the disciples, Jesus said, "Don't you understand this parable? How then will you understand any parable?" (verse 13).

Commenting on this a few verses later, Jesus underlines the main point for us: "Consider carefully what you hear" (verse 24). *That is the key.* This book is about hearing and obeying the commands of Jesus. So it is good to treat this seventh command first. You cannot obey what you have not heard. It has always been that way. Jesus told the disciples numerous times that they had to listen. God the Father jumped in on that message, for example, during the Transfiguration when He said to the disciples: "This is my Son, whom I love; with him I am well pleased. *Listen to him!*" (Matthew 17:5).

The makeup of words themselves often conveys important meaning. The Latin "to hear" is the word *oboedire,* from which we derive the English word *obey.* The idea is that if you truly hear you will obey. Obedience is the indication that we have heard.

When approaching the Lord to listen to Him, it might be good to keep in mind who He is. While He is the sovereign Creator of the universe (immense), He knows the number of hairs on your head (miniscule). He has all knowledge and all wisdom and all love, so He knows what you need and how you need it, and He wants to give it to you.

One of the things we need to get over is the fear that He will send us to China if we ask for direction. He has sent me to China—four times so far—and it was a hoot each time. I had a ball! But you know what I mean: We are afraid to ask God for direction because we might not like the answer. But He already knows that, doesn't He? So why not just 'fess up and tell Him? "Sometimes I do not want to ask for Your input, Lord, because I am afraid I will not like Your answer." Go ahead and tell Him that. I mean, if He is God, can't He handle your fear? Even your fear of Him? Hello?

When we refuse to listen to Him, we are effectively telling Him He is not trustworthy—or that we are not trustworthy to obey. In either case, He is debilitated and we are flying solo. That does not work so well. Tell you what: Just go ahead and tell God right now how you feel about listening to and obeying Him. Do not hold back. Remember, He already knows what you are thinking, so you might as well come clean.

God's Problem in Speaking

God has decided that He and you collaborate through the primary dynamic of faith. And while He has decided that you take action on what He says as an act of your will, He does not speak to your will when He is talking. Rather, He talks to your spirit. From there you must translate His words to your mind and your emotions. Your will must assess what He has said while taking input from your mind and emotions, and then finally you decide to take action or inaction. Some of the stories I will tell illustrate this process.

The difficulty comes in the strength with which He speaks. God's *modus operandi* for us is stated in Hebrews: "Without faith it is impossible to please God, because anyone who comes to him must believe that he exists and that he rewards those who earnestly seek him" (Hebrews 11:6). What that means is that you do not get to be sure of what He is saying prior to the need to take action on what He has said. You operate either in faith or certainty but not both at the same time. If you are positive about something, you do not need faith, do you? Faith is needed when it is possible and even probable that God is saying to do something, but you are not sure about it.

If God spoke so loudly that there was no doubt about something, faith would not be necessary. But He wants us to have faith. Faith is the coin of His realm. It is what frees Him to work. This is not mechanical—He is not a vending machine—but personal. Faith is being persuaded that He wants you to do something, but persuasion is not certainty.

So God's problem is how to speak loudly enough that we hear but not so loudly that we have no doubt. Do not ask me why He works this way. I do not particularly like it, but I am resigned that it is the way the God business goes. I am never completely at ease when I am hearing and obeying Him. But this forces me into a greater dependence on Him, and I have found that dependence on Him is always profitable. We have a right to orders, but we do not seem to have a right for them to be barked at us.

Our Problem in Listening

I have asserted that God is canny enough to speak without overpowering us with His messages. But we do not want to run off half-cocked and do a bunch of stupid things just because it *may* have been God speaking. Do we? So how do we manage this business of being open to God for His direction while needing some measure of assurance that it really is He who is talking to us?

First, it is important to realize and remember that we should put our emphasis on Him rather than us. If He is who the Bible says He is, He knows everything about us—genes, education, experiences, temperament, influences, intelligence, etc. So He knows how to talk to us. Trust that! Do not trust your ability to hear Him; rather, trust His ability to speak to you. That will keep the focus on Him, where it is safe.

Then, realize that He speaks in a wide variety of ways: through Scripture, nature, the supernatural, circumstances and other people. We will look briefly at each of these ways.

Finally, it is good to realize that He knows our need for some assurance. Confirmation is the means He gives for assurance. One means of guidance will confirm another, and from that confirmation we can take confidence.

Okay, let's look at the ways He speaks to us.

Scripture

The Scriptures are the clearest form of guidance God has provided us. They are also the checker-outer of other kinds of guidance. But using the Scriptures is not easy or simple. Being too literal and being too liberal are approaches to the Scriptures that ignore the Holy Spirit. A good principle to remember is that it took the Holy Spirit to *write* Scripture, and it takes the Holy Spirit to *read* Scripture and *interpret* it correctly.

Two key passages address the importance of interpreting Scripture correctly. "Above all, you must understand that no prophecy of Scripture came about by the prophet's own interpretation. For prophecy never had its origin in the will of man, but men spoke from God as they were carried along by the Holy Spirit" (2 Peter 1:20–21). And Hebrews 4:12: "For the word of God is living and active. Sharper than any double-edged sword, it penetrates even to dividing soul and spirit, joints and marrow; it judges the thoughts and attitudes of the heart."

These verses can direct us to a three-part attitude toward Scripture. First, our hearts should respect, appreciate and fear the Bible. Second, we should maintain an expectation of Scripture's ability to bring light, conviction and training. Third, we must have enough humility to expose our interpretations of Scripture to others for their agreement or correction. These attitudes will eliminate 98 percent of the mistakes people make reading the Bible.

Generally, it helps to read Scripture in macro and micro ways. First, we should read large portions of it in order to fill our understanding with God's opinion of various matters. The more we read Scripture, the more we begin to think like God, evaluate matters from His perspective and judge things from His stance. Often it is helpful to read everything the Bible says about a given subject. A concordance can direct you to the various places that address a particular subject.

Second, we should be ready for the Lord to underline specific passages He wants us to apply to our lives at the time. Thirty years ago I was doing the first kind of reading, plowing through the Bible's treatment of the poor. Suddenly these words jumped off the page at me: "I was a stranger and you invited me in" (Matthew 25:35). I knew that those words meant to take in street people and I did not want to do that, so I read on—faster—pretending that those words had not affected me.

The next day a social worker came into my office, introduced herself and said, "I have a problem that perhaps you could help me with. I have a sixteen-year-old boy in my charge who is homeless. He breaks into cars on used car lots at night in order to sleep safely in the seats." Then, looking me straight in the eye, she said, "Will you take him in?"

That blasted passage from Scripture blazed into my consciousness, of course, but I still did not want to take in street people, so I fumbled around and mentioned that I could not make any decision until I had spoken with my wife. That bought me a bit of time. The social worker handed me her card and asked me to call when I made up my mind.

As Sue and I talked it over that evening, we could think of all the reasons *not* to take him in. I will not elaborate on them here—you fill in the blanks. And God was utterly silent about our what-ifs.

But in opposition to all our reasonable resistance was that underlined phrase, "I was a stranger and you took me in." I knew the possibility that God was inviting us to take in strangers was stronger than the possibility that He was not asking this of us. So the next day, I took out the social worker's card, dialed her up and said, "Bring him over." They were there in fifteen minutes.

The boy stayed with us for a year. He was the first of more than 120 persons whom the Lord led us to take in over the next twenty years. It would take the rest of this book to tell you what blessings have come to my family and me because we obeyed that passage of Scripture. Incidentally, note that I received confirmation in the matter: The social worker's visit confirmed the underlined reading of the passage just the day before.

I would encourage you to adopt Jesus' attitude toward Scripture, which He quoted or referred to 47 times in the gospels. An open reading of the gospels shows that Jesus believed:

- in Noah and the flood story (Matthew 24:36–39)
- in hell (Mark 9:47, quoting Isaiah 66:24)
- that fire and sulfur rained down from heaven on Sodom (Luke 17:26–29)
- that Moses actually encountered the burning bush (Luke 20:37)

In other words, Jesus seemed to have no trouble believing the veracity of Scripture or the events that Scripture relates.

Over and over as He spoke to the disciples, He asserted, "The Scriptures must be fulfilled" (for instance, Mark 14:49). He saw Himself as the fulfillment of all the messianic prophecies. This attitude enabled Him to realize that David was speaking of Him in the puzzling "The Lord said to my Lord" passage (Matthew 22:41–46). To launch His ministry He read from the portions of Isaiah that predicted the things He would do. Then He said

He was the One. And then He proved it by doing the things that had been foretold.

If language means anything at all, we must conclude that Jesus held an attitude toward Scripture that includes these points:

- He saw Scripture as God's Word.
- Scripture outlined the ministry He was to exercise.
- Scripture was the compendium containing God's position on all matters.
- Scripture was believable.
- Scripture was to be obeyed.

Jesus continually resorted to Scripture to support His claims, verify His arguments and defeat His opponents. I would encourage you to think about Scripture just as He did.

And I would encourage you to expose yourself to God's directions to you through Scripture. One day, for example, these words leaped off the page and into my mind: "Owe no man any thing, but to love one another" (Romans 13:8, KJV). Well, I owed the credit card people all kinds of money. As my wife and I considered this, we realized God wanted us to cut up all our credit cards and to trust that He would bring in enough money for our needs. We felt insecure about that but did it anyway. God richly blessed us. And in six months we were out of debt. That was a great benefit to us.

Nature

As the Author and Sustainer of nature, God knows how to speak to us through it. St. Paul claims that anyone with eyes ought to be able to realize from looking at nature that there is a God who created it (Romans 1:20). Nature is reality and God is real, so He likes speaking through it.

Many of Jesus' parables had a natural backdrop. I mentioned His analogy of building on rock or on sand to make the point that we must obey His teachings. It is easy to get that point. The same is true in the parable of the sower: We each can identify with the three negative ways and the one positive way of responding to the Word of God that has been sown in our lives.

Once a month I take a full day to hear the Lord. I almost always go to nature—the mountains, the seaside, a valley. Frequently the Lord speaks to me through the natural things I observe and experience. Sometimes the message is purely natural, as when I notice a bird being sustained by the wind and realize that the wind of God—the Holy Spirit—will sustain me if I spread the wings of faith. Sometimes the message is supernatural. Once, for example, in a time of feeling worthless I asked the Lord to part the clouds and let the sun shine on me if He thought I was worth anything. He did so within two minutes.

Examine nature. You will find God's teachings in it for you.

The Supernatural

God also speaks to us in supernatural ways. Elijah, you remember, heard the Lord in "a gentle whisper" (1 Kings 19:12). He was way up on a mountain in a cave. On this occasion the Lord did not speak through nature—the wind, the earthquake, the fire—though He caused these things. Rather, He spoke through a still, small voice, which Elijah could hear because he was alone with the Lord. This example is very characteristic of how the Lord speaks today. My joke about it is, "He speaks in a 'whis,' which is half a whisper."

How does one hear that "whis"? First, we must realize how He speaks. It has been my experience that the Lord speaks in a variety of ways:[1]

1. Pictures
2. An inner knowing
3. A picture of a written word

4. A spontaneous utterance that comes without your volition
5. A memory of something that happened to you or another person
6. A concept or impression
7. A commonsense observation
8. A pain in your body that indicates His desire to heal someone else with that condition
9. A rush of compassion

But it must be said again that all of these impressions are generally quite slight. They do not hang in your consciousness for detailed examination. Rather they pass through like dim shooting stars.

Next, it is good to have some sense of what it feels like to receive this kind of supernatural input. The Scriptures call this kind of input from God "message of knowledge" (1 Corinthians 12:8). Words of knowledge—and all spiritual gifts—usually feel quite natural when one is operating in them. They do not feel "spiritual" or "electric." Rather, they feel quite normal. In fact, through thoughts and feelings our enemy often tries to tell us we are lying or making up words of knowledge. The only way we can know if the word is genuine is to speak it out and act on it. Therefore risk is an unavoidable factor in receiving and expressing the word of knowledge, which, incidentally, is another reason why faith is an act of the will rather than of the intellect or the emotions.

It also is helpful to realize that words of knowledge fit the personality or temperament types of those receiving them. God has created all types of people and knows how to speak to each of them individually. You must never insist that He speak to you the way He speaks to someone else, for we are made differently. If a person is strongly visual, words of knowledge will probably work in a visual way for him or her. Strongly conceptual people usually will have impressions. Those with a strong tendency toward common sense will feel that the word of knowledge seems like simple common sense. In other words, the Holy Spirit tailors the manner of giving the word of knowledge to fit the makeup of each individual person.

The next thing to do is relax. If we are so focused on hearing Him that we are all tied up and stressed out, we will not hear anything. Heavy concentration is not what allows His messages to come through. This is why people often hear the Lord when they least expect, such as in the shower or while driving—anytime the mind is not strongly focused. Relaxing is what opens us to Him. So you just dial down your thoughts, your emotions, your body and your actions. Then you wait with a sense of light expectancy that the Lord will speak.

I would like to share with you some suggestions on hearing God that are based upon my experience:

- Walking works well for me.
- Sitting quietly may be your style.
- Consciously refuse to concentrate on anything.
- Pray for a few seconds in tongues, if you exercise a prayer language.
- Pay attention to what comes to mind—do not examine it too quickly, but just let the rest come.
- Always check what you hear with Scripture. Does it sound like the way God dealt with people in the Bible? Does it coincide with the teachings of Scripture?
- Consider: Do you have peace about this word of knowledge? Does it seem like God to you? Is it reasonable? Do-able? Does it meet the need?

Some years ago I led a mission to Argentina. In the Anglican cathedral in Buenos Aires, we saw God heal many people through us and our prayers. But when we went to the interior province of Cordoba, our prayers seemed totally fruitless. We did not see anyone healed. After a day of failure, I went on a morning walk around the large ranch where I was staying. I enjoyed the birds, the vast rolling hills and the herds of cattle.

41

After quieting down sufficiently, I asked the Lord why no one in this area was being healed. In that "whis" I mentioned previously, a single, soft word came into my consciousness: *curandero*. I saw it printed lightly in my mind just long enough to read it. I did not know what it meant, so I asked my host. He informed me that curanderos are folk healers to whom the locals take their children when they have upset stomachs and the like.

"What does the curandero do?" I asked.

"Oh, they take a string of beads and make an 'X' across the chest of the child and mumble some words. Maybe they give him an amulet to wear. We take the child home and in a while he is well."

Suddenly I realized that the curandero was lifting one condition only to impose an occultic influence over the children. The parents, believing that the curandero, a type of witch doctor, had magical powers, continued to bring the patient back to him. As the curandero was paid for his services, the cash kept coming in, of course, but the child was not really healed. In fact, the presence of occultic influences actually was preventing people from receiving God's healing, as God considers it a sin to engage in any occult practices. From that point on, we encouraged the sick to repent of having gone or been taken to a curandero and to renounce his influence. It is through renouncement of the occult that the door is opened once again to God's healing power. Soon after, healing broke out just as it had in Buenos Aires. One man in his early seventies had been ill most of his life, but he was symptom free within moments of having renounced the curanderos.

My willingness to hear God that day enabled many people to receive healing and come to know Christ. Hundreds more received healing and salvation after we left as our hosts followed our lead. Hearing God is tremendously important because it permits God to do all the other things He wants to do to or through us.

In Scripture, the word of knowledge has a number of purposes:

- It reveals sin.
  1. Nathan to David—2 Samuel 12:1–7 (verse 7)
  2. Elisha to Gehazi—2 Kings 5:20–27 (verse 26)
  3. Jesus to the woman at the well—John 4:7–25 (verse 17)
  4. Peter to Ananias—Acts 5:1–6 (verse 2)
- It helps to find something.
  1. Samuel to Saul—1 Samuel 9:15–20 (verse 20)
  2. Samuel to Saul—1 Samuel 10:22
- It warns and provides safety.
  —Elisha to the king of Israel—2 Kings 6:8–23 (verse 9)
- It reveals thoughts.
  —Jesus to the scribes—Matthew 9:1–7 (verse 4)
- It provides healing.
  1. Jesus and the paralytic—Matthew 9:1–7
  2. Jesus and the man who was ill 38 years—John 5:1–9 (verse 6)

At the time of this writing I have just returned from a mission to Brazil, where I experienced a healing that is a good example of collaborating with the Lord. During one ministry time a dear lady, about 78 years old, came forward seeking prayer for depression. I started to tell her we could not do much in that setting because depression requires a style of prayer called inner healing, which takes quite a bit of time. All this was through an interpreter. But out of habit I checked with the Lord. He told me to ask her *why* she was depressed. She replied that her sight had deteriorated ten months ago.

"That is why you're depressed?" I asked.

"Yes," was the reply.

"What can you see?"

"The floor."

"Let's pray for your sight." So I asked the Holy Spirit to visit her. After a minute I asked if she detected any change. She looked around and said, "I can see people now, but I can't see their faces." So we prayed for another minute.

"Now I can see their eyes," she said, and she left in the joy of Jesus.

Circumstances

When God speaks through circumstances, He is pulling strings. When He wants you to do something, He often arranges circumstances in your life to confirm the direction or decision He wants. You experience doors closing that you cannot close or doors opening that you cannot open. Once again, the Lord does not clobber you with His input. But if you are looking for confirmation, you may find it in circumstances.

A few years ago I felt the Lord leading me to write a short book on disciple making. But none of the publishers I approached about the project were interested in a short book. Several, in fact, urged me to turn it into a full-sized book, indicating it would be more attractive that way. But each time, I felt the Lord saying, *No, keep it short. A big book says, "This is complicated," by sheer virtue of its length. I want people to know that anyone can make disciples. Keep it short.* So I was between the Rock and the hard place.

Suddenly I was given the opportunity to print it with several 62-page books that John Wimber, my mentor, was publishing. This was the answer. I adjusted it so that it would take up 62 pages, and it was printed. God was at work in those circumstances, publishing the book in the format He wanted.

Other People

Other people have wisdom, insight and perspective that we need. Christianity is not a solo flight, so we need to avail ourselves of others' input. This is especially true in decisions that have long-term consequences, such as getting married, changing jobs or moving to a different state. When confronted with the need to make a major decision, ask the Lord whom He would have you consult.

Often others see us more clearly than we see ourselves. Once I was offered a position in a church where I did not want to go. But as I consulted other mature Christians, their opinion was that it would be a good match. God used those opinions to confirm other things He was doing to direct me to accept that position. I did accept it, and over the next fourteen years God used that congregation to do wonderful things for His Kingdom, both domestically and internationally. By His grace and because of experiences like that one, God has been able to use me to prevent a number of other people from making big mistakes because of wise counsel He told me to share with them.

The book of Proverbs gives several pieces of wisdom about seeking advice:

"For lack of guidance a nation falls, but many advisers make victory sure" (11:14).

"The way of a fool seems right to him, but a wise man listens to advice" (12:15).

"Pride only breeds quarrels, but wisdom is found in those who take advice" (13:10).

"Plans fail for lack of counsel, but with many advisers they succeed" (15:22).

Peace and Surprise Thinking

A couple of additional factors can bring us some assurance. One is inner peace. As you consider taking a course of action, pause to sense the level of your peace about it. In my experience, peace is perceived as stillness in the center of my chest, which I suspect is the dwelling place of the human spirit. If I am not peaceful about something, I have learned that it is not wise to overrule that dis-ease. "Let the peace of Christ rule in your hearts," Paul says to the Colossians (3:15). Peace is the final thing I check before taking action.

In major decisions, Scripture, circumstance, agreement of other mature Christians and my peace all must line up in favor of the proposed course of action. If even one of those is in disagreement, I wait until all agree.

In minor matters I rely mostly upon peace and surprise thinking. By this I mean things that pop into my mind that I would not have thought of. Moses indicated that this was a factor he used in decision making: "This is how you will know that the LORD has sent me to do all these things and that *it was not my idea*" (Numbers 16:28). I know my mind pretty well, and I can usually determine pretty quickly if I would have conceived the thoughts that occur. If I know the thought did not come from my own mental process, then I am usually pretty confident that the thought is from the Lord. Often I have found that taking action on those surprise thoughts turns out well. I must add, however, that my use of peace and surprise thinking is backed up by a rather thorough knowledge of Scripture, which I have read through at least 25 times. So I am always able to immediately balance the thought against the standard of Scripture. I encourage you to be able to do the same.

God Is Eager to Speak

Scripture, nature, the supernatural, circumstances and other people are various means that God uses to give us direction. Confirmation is the dynamic by which God gives us assurance of His guidance while still relying on faith. And peace and surprise thinking give us reassurance that what we believe we are hearing from God is correct and true.

God is eager to speak to you. This is why "Listen!" is one of the top seven commands of Jesus. And if you make it your determination to listen to Him, you will surely start being aware of His messages to you.

3

The Sixth Command: *Grow Up*

"My Goodness Shows as You Grow Up in Me"

Crossing lines between languages can reveal interesting and enlightening facts about the meanings of words. We use the word *character* in English. Its Greek rendition spelled with the English alphabet is *karakter*. The literal meaning of this word in Greek bears a striking demonstration of what character truly is. It refers to the imprint made on pliable material by a signet ring. So the mark put on clay or wax is the character of the ring.

In the opening verses of the book of Hebrews, Jesus is extolled in these terms: "The Son is the radiance of God's glory and the *exact representation* of his being, sustaining all things by his powerful word" (Hebrews 1:3). The words *exact representation* are a translation of this Greek word *karakter*. Other translations use these phrases: "the very stamp of his nature," "the express image of his person" and "the very imprint of his being." So when we look at Jesus we observe the imprint of the Father's essence, His nature, His character. You could say that Jesus is the character of God, the imprint of God. And He, in fact, said something very like that to Philip: "Anyone who has seen me has seen the Father" (John 14:9).

It is important for us to realize that just as Jesus discloses the Father, we are to disclose Jesus. People will notice the essence, nature and character of Jesus when they look at us. I am serious. And I challenge you to be serious about this. Jesus wants you to look like Him, act like Him and sound like Him.

Jesus Discloses God; We Disclose Jesus

The following chart compares Jesus' relationship with the Father to your relationship with Jesus in the gospel of John. Note that Jesus is the speaker in each instance:

The Father and Jesus	Jesus and You
"I tell you the truth, the Son can do nothing by himself; he can do only what he sees his Father doing" (5:19).	"Apart from me you can do nothing" (15:5).
"As the Father has loved me" (15:9).	"So have I loved you" (15:9).
"...just as I have obeyed my Father's commands and remain in his love" (15:10).	"If you obey my commands, you will remain in my love" (15:10).
"Do not believe me unless I do what my Father does" (10:37).	"I tell you the truth, anyone who has faith in me will do what I have been doing" (14:12).
"Whoever accepts me accepts the one who sent me" (13:20).	"Whoever accepts anyone I send accepts me" (13:20).
"On that day you will realize that I am in my Father" (14:20, also verse 10).	"You are in me, and I am in you" (14:20).
"...and you in me" (17:23).	"I in them..." (17:23).
"You gave me [the words]" (17:8).	"For I gave them the words... and they accepted them" (17:8).
"As the Father has sent me..." (20:21).	"...I am sending you" (20:21).

Looking at each column of statements, it is easy to see that Jesus' relationship with the Father is the model for our relationship with Jesus:

- As Jesus was helpless without the Father, we are helpless without Jesus.
- As Jesus obeyed the Father, we are to obey Jesus.
- As the Father was in Jesus, Jesus is to be in us.
- As Jesus was sent by the Father, we are to be sent by Jesus.
- As the Father acted through Jesus, Jesus is to act through us.

So there is a daunting challenge and a glorious promise in these comparisons. The challenge is that we are to look and act like Jesus. The promise is that He will empower us to do it.

St. Paul echoes these thoughts in 1 Corinthians 3:23: "And you are of Christ, and Christ is of God." Let's summarize this relationship in a kind of equation:

As the Father is to the Son, so is the Son to the believer.

What Does It Mean to Grow Up?

To grow up means to look and behave like Jesus. As He perfectly displayed the nature and character of the Father, so we are to improve more and more in displaying His nature and character. The difficulty comes in trying to learn *how* to display Him. That "how" is not the easiest thing to understand or live out.

The command to grow up encompasses many of the commands of Jesus that pertain to maturity. Some of them are:

- Be salt (Matthew 5:13).
- Let your light shine (Matthew 5:16).
- Do not be angry (Matthew 5:22).
- Do not look with lust (Matthew 5:28).
- Do not swear (Matthew 5:34).

- Be perfect (Matthew 5:48).
- Judge not (Matthew 7:1).
- Do not divorce (Matthew 19:9).
- Humble yourself (Luke 14:10).
- Have a good heart (Luke 6:45).
- Do not worry (Matthew 6:25).
- Be poor in spirit, mourn, be meek, thirst for righteousness, be merciful, be pure in heart, be peacemakers, be persecuted for righteousness, rejoice when persecuted (the Beatitudes, Matthew 5:3–12).
- Lose your life in order to gain it (Matthew 16:24–26).
- Deny yourself, take up your cross, follow Jesus (Luke 9:23).
- Abide in Me (John 15:4).
- Bear much fruit (John 15:8).

Our difficulty comes as we rely on ourselves to produce those behaviors of maturity. And I have observed that most people first try to do it themselves. Something about us just assumes that we can do what is expected. We have a most kind and patient God who lets us attempt first by ourselves what only He can enable us to do.

My Experience in Growing Up

As I have said, one of my favorite slogans is that a servant has a right to orders. In my own experience, I came to Jesus for orders—

He gave them.
I went out to obey them.
I failed, and He forgave me.
I came to Jesus for orders.

50

He gave them again.
I went out to obey them.
I failed, and He forgave me.
I came to Jesus for orders.
He gave them again.
I went out to obey them.
I failed, and He forgave me.

I could write this sequence hundreds of times, couldn't I? Couldn't you?

The Lord was waiting for me to come to a new mind-set that would be born of a humble heart. For what He means to accomplish out of our many failures is the humility to allow Him to do the work in us. Until humility comes, we simply fail miserably while trying to do it ourselves. My attitude was, "I'll do it myself, thank you very much. Don't I have a good intellect, a good education, a backlog of experiences? I can do what needs to be done!"

So the Lord kindly removed His hand from me—I would not have accepted it anyway—and let me blunder on. I was overdue for change, but He let me blunder on, waiting for the moment when my own incapacity to grow up would be undeniable even to one as blind as I.

Then in the spring of 1972 I attended a denominational conference. A friend and I were late to one of the dinner sessions, so we took a shortcut to the meeting hall. As we pulled on a side door to enter, we realized it was locked. But what luck! A doorman was just on the other side. Through the glass we said to him, "Could you let us in?"

"No," he replied, "you'll have to go around to the main door."

"But we belong in there," we answered.

"Sorry, sir."

"See our name tags? They are the same as those at those tables."

"Sorry, sir, you'll have to go around."

In fury, I turned around and launched my foot back at the door to rattle it in protest at his obstinacy. But it shattered. I numbed into shock. In just seconds the rent-a-cops were escorting me to the convention manager's office. As I stood before him I realized that I could be arrested for vandalism. But my anger prevented me from humbly appealing to him. I threw my business card on his desk shouting that I would pay for his blankety-blank door.

He looked at the card and said, "You're a priest and you kicked in our door." It was not an accusation; rather, it was the mind of a man straining to grasp two facts. He said it again, more assertively, as though assertion would bring clarity: "You're a priest and you kicked in our door." But he was not putting those two facts together very well. This was a graceful man trying to comprehend an ungraceful act. Finally he looked at me and said, "Okay, I'll send you a bill," and I escaped from his office.

But I could not escape from self-accusation. The act of kicking in a convention center door was outside my view of myself. For five months I ran to the hills whenever I could, stomping back and forth across their brows, repeating, "I cannot believe I kicked in that door!" I found myself saying, "If I could do *that,* what else might I do?" And I feared for myself and those around me. Slowly, I began to get honest about myself. It was slow because I saw no light at the end of the tunnel. It is hard to admit that you are in hell if you have no vision of heaven—or that you are in darkness when you have no view of light.

The immediate result was depression. But God had a better result in mind and waited for the right moment. I have told part of this story in a previous book, *Holy Vulnerability,*[1] and I do not believe it necessary to repeat myself here. Let me just say that the Lord arranged for me to encounter a book that had the answer to my immediate need. I did not especially like the answer when I saw it, as it involved the Lord's promise of empowerment by the Holy Spirit. To me it sounded weird. I had aspirations of becoming a high-ranking clergyman in my denomination, and getting involved in "weird" Christianity just would not get me there. But my need—and the honesty to admit it—was greater than my hopes for my career.

As I learned about the power of the Holy Spirit, I discovered that it makes available to Jesus' followers two categories of His resources: His abilities—called gifts—and His character—called fruit. For the purposes of this chapter, it is the fruit that I wish to address.

I read that in Galatians 5 Paul lists the fruit of the flesh: "sexual immorality, impurity and debauchery; idolatry and witchcraft; hatred, discord, jealousy, fits of rage, selfish ambition, dissensions, factions and envy; drunkenness, orgies and the like. I warn you, as I did before, that those who live like this will not inherit the kingdom of God" (verses 19–21). I could identify with at least three of those.

By contrast, Paul goes on, "The fruit of the Spirit is love, joy, peace, patience, kindness, goodness, faithfulness, gentleness and self-control" (Galatians 5:22). Those were the qualities I desperately needed. The Lord was saying that Jesus' ownership of these qualities was available to me through the operation of the Holy Spirit if I would ask.

Finally, finally, I had the humility to ask for and receive them. I caved in to the Lord's promise and asked for empowerment by His Spirit. It happened for me on August 22, 1972.

The first step is having the humility to admit that we cannot model Christ on our own. Then we must ask God for the empowerment of His Holy Spirit to help us. Only then can we begin to look more like Christ. If you are interested—and I recommend that you be interested—you might look over the teaching notes on baptism with the Holy Spirit in Appendix B. For the empowerment of the Holy Spirit is the key to growing up in Christ.

Maturity Comes through the Holy Spirit

After asking for the empowerment of the Holy Spirit, I noticed two things about maturity. First, I had been way overdue for some of Jesus' qualities. Quickly my temper gave way to self-control, my impurity succumbed to the ability to resist the temptation to look at pornography, my cynicism was replaced by hope and my anxieties were exchanged for the peace of Jesus. Those things happened within days of August 22. And while I still had periodic bouts with fleshly fruit, the Lord had delivered me from being in utter bondage to them.

Second, over the years that followed the Lord has confronted other maturity issues when He thought it was time for me to grow up in reference to them—or when I got honest enough to acknowledge that I needed His help in order to grow up in them—or both. The business of growing up into the fullness of the measure of the stature of Christ, as Paul outlines it (Ephesians 4:12–13), is a process rather than an event. One quality of maturity provides the foundation for another, and that for yet another. You do not just get there all at once. Nonetheless, there is urgency about maturing in Christ. John Wimber wrote, "Over the course of more than twenty years in the ministry, I have become convinced that one of the most important things any of us can do as a Christian is to *grow up before we grow old.* It is absolutely essential, if we are to make progress in the great enterprise of helping men and women find redemption, that we see growth toward maturity as part of our goal—both for them and for ourselves."[2]

How do you grow up in Christ? Well, there are two sides to the answer: God's side and man's side. God meticulously influences your life, arranging needs, opportunities and challenges in exquisite detail and care. From your side, Paul's advice is pertinent: "Those who belong to Christ Jesus have crucified the sinful nature with its passions and desires. Since we live by the Spirit, let us keep in step with the Spirit" (Galatians 5:24–25). How do you crucify the sinful nature? In two ways. First, you begin to identify yourself with Jesus when He was on the cross dying for your sins and to understand that the sinful you was killed when Jesus died. Read that sentence again. Second, you say no to the things your flesh wants you to do, relying on the Holy Spirit to actualize and administrate your no.

How do you enact that you died when Jesus died? If I could just tell you and you could just understand it, that would be nice. But reality at this level is not very simple. God has designed things so that the *how* is lived before it is understood. In fact, it is the living that allows the understanding to occur. You *do* it, and that enables you to *understand* it; but even then, the doing exceeds the understanding. How do you do it? You act—in thought and attitude and action—as if the thing were true. You act as if the sinful you died when Jesus died and the obedient you was raised when He was raised. You act as if the Spirit will back up your no to the flesh and keep you from behaving in accord with its wishes. You act as if you are following Jesus the Pure, Jesus the Mature.

You act as if He is in you and you are in Him. You act as if He knows how to live His own life in you. You act as if He is who He says He is and you are who He says you are.

"Well, isn't that just an act?" you might exclaim. Sure it is. But do not let your opinion of "just an act" sabotage the biblical view that *acting as if* is exactly what faith is. Jesus provided the clue in John 7:17: "If anyone chooses to do God's will, he will find out whether my teaching comes from God or whether I speak on my own." In other words, doing precedes comprehending. This is not acting as if something false were true. It is releasing the truth into actuality by taking steps that prove its truthfulness.

Why is this important? Because it allows you to be blessed and to be a blessing. God loves you and wants blessing for you and through you.

At the time of this writing, I just celebrated the thirtieth anniversary of my infilling with the Spirit. Almost daily I gush with gratitude to God for giving me the opportunity to be filled with His Spirit. My level of happiness must be hundreds times more than it would have been had I not been filled. My usefulness, my inner peace, my relationships, my ability to collaborate effectively with the Lord Jesus—all these are vastly more healthy and fulsome than they would have been otherwise. By God! I am growing up. Or rather, by God I am growing up. It is by God that I am maturing. Even at 62 years of age, I have nothing in and of myself to offer Him or anyone else.

As an old saint, Norman Grubb, pointed out, "I learned then to change from the false idea of becoming something to containing Someone."[3] As I seek to contain and give forth the Lord Jesus, somehow He mobilizes the best of me-in-Him and sends both of us forth from me for others. It is the most amazing free-flow collaboration. As I try to give Him forth, He likes sounding like me. It is not that I diminish in the act of giving forth Jesus. Rather, it is that He enlarges me or intensifies what it is to be me and gladly wears me—my body, my personality, my vocabulary—as I seek to relate with others in Him. I cannot die to self fast enough to stay dead, for He is too quick in the raising of me. He likes me alive!

Jesus Christ is the same, yesterday, today and forever, as the Book says (Hebrews 13:8). But He is infinitely unique and modulated as He expresses Himself in each of us, for we all are different. He likes sounding like me and He likes sounding like you *when* each of us is seeking to contain and give Him forth to others. This is not only great fun. It is what is called maturity. As the subtitle of this chapter asserts, *My goodness shows as you grow up in Me.* Jesus is the character of the Father. You are meant to be the character of Jesus.

Growing Up in Christ Is Not Always Fun

But this business of growing up is not always fun. At times it is difficult, such as when you see the cost but do not yet see the reward. On such occasions, the word *integrity* is central. There is much to tempt us away from integrity: saving face, saving money, saving reputation, saving time, even saving friendships. At such times the command to exhibit integrity seems oversimplified, insensitive and costly.

One day a lawyer was waiting in my office when I returned from lunch. As I entered, he slapped a suit in my hands. I was blindsided, unable to think or to master my emotions. I stumbled into church and went up to the altar. Laying the suit papers on the altar, I looked up. Then I heard the words from Isaiah 53:7: "He did not open his mouth; he was led like a lamb to the slaughter, and as a sheep before her shearers is silent, so he did not open his mouth." This passage prophesied Jesus' behavior during His trials. And the Lord said, "You may not defend yourself in this matter. Keep silent."

In the five months it took to resolve the case, there were many times when I yearned to speak out and defend myself. My name was splashed across the headlines of several large newspapers. When reporters called to get my side of the matter, I had to be quiet. Even friends and long-term parishioners looked sideways at me, as though the charges might be true. And I could tell them nothing. I was relearning that faith is not an act of intellect or of emotions but of *will*, for my mind found all kinds of reasons to speak up, and my emotions were in riot at what people thought of me. It was only by the will that I refrained from speaking. The Lord strengthened my will on several occasions when I was sorely tempted to disobey His injunction. Somehow He got me through that period.

The day after the case was resolved, I saw these words from Psalm 35 in my daily Bible reading:

> Ruthless witnesses come forward; they question me on things I know nothing about. They repay me evil for good and leave my soul forlorn. Yet when they were ill, I put on sackcloth and humbled myself with fasting. When my prayers returned to me unanswered, I went about mourning as though for my friend or brother. I bowed my head in grief as though weeping for my mother.
>
> verses 11–14

57

As I read those words, the Lord said in my mind, *You have not done that for your enemy.* I was aghast and exclaimed, "What kind of God are You? That person tried to destroy my ministry!" But a couple of days later I decided to fast and pray for my enemy. A single day of fasting and praying freed me from all anger and bitterness toward my enemy. I was freed to pray for and bless and wish for that person's well-being.

In the years since then, I have thanked God for that trial. He used it to strengthen my integrity and to prepare me for other challenging occasions. Because of having kept silent, some cord of strength in me was ready for the next challenge.

Now, my friend, what challenges has the Lord allowed to come your way? What in His Word has He said to you about them? May I urge you to do what He has said? Your world is desperate to see Jesus. In you. It is about integrity.

Individual Responsibility

Many years ago I told a little white lie in the process of witnessing to someone I was trying to lead to Jesus. It did not work, and the person remained unconverted. Later, the Lord spoke to me: *I cannot use a lie, Mike, even one designed to bring Me into someone's heart.* I have tried to maintain rigorous honesty ever since.

Honesty is recognition of the truth and behavior consonant with the truth. Overruling the excuses for dishonesty is part of integrity development. A wonderful result of exercising the faith to maintain integrity is that the Lord gives us resolutions of problems and rewards for obedience that we could never have gained on our own.

Honesty requires a distinction between mercy and repayment. Abe Lincoln borrowed a book that was ruined by the rain. He worked it off at 25 cents a day until it was paid for. Too often today, *mercy* is translated as meaning that repayment is canceled.

To whom do you owe something? What are you going to do about it?

In the final analysis, what you *do* is your gift to the world. But doing flows out of being. It is who you *are* that produces action. It is what you and God make of yourself. Who you are determines what you will be able to do.

The Importance of Accountability

Individual integrity is nearly impossible without the help of friends. Accountability in the church is an opportunity to grow through a relationship that no other relationship on earth provides. No other relationship provides the combination of grace, honesty, forgiveness, forbearance, hope and power that accountability among believers can provide.

The goal of accountability is not success but growth, not perfection but improvement, not flying solo but being part of the flock. Accountability suggests the lateral, horizontal aspect of life. When we are accountable to other people, we *count* to them—we matter—and we count *to them*—we itemize our actions. We give them authority in relation to our lives. And we trust and respect those to whom we are accountable.

Following is a list of the benefits and characteristics of accountability:

- Accountability presupposes love and acceptance. You must know that the person loves you before you will hold yourself accountable to him or her.
- Accountability presupposes a desire to be well.
- Accountability presupposes a determination to relate.
- Accountability requires honesty, trust and courage in the one being held accountable.
- Accountability requires trustworthiness, discretion and largeness of heart in those holding a person accountable.

- Accountability promotes balance, health and intimacy.
- Accountability is not a relationship of adversaries but of companions.
- Accountability holds us to God's standard in areas of sin, makes us responsible for agreed-upon criteria, keeps us maturing and keeps us healthy.
- Accountability allows us to be agents of each other's growth and freedom.
- Accountability recognizes that none of us is a capable judge of ourselves.
- Accountability provides an ongoing opportunity to get real, to become truthful, to face our spiritual enemies and to lay hold of the grace to change what should be changed.
- Accountability says, "I give you permission to ask tough questions." For example: "Have you done what you said you were going to do?" "Why?" "Why not?" "Have you just lied to me?"

I encourage you to become accountable. Select a close friend who is the same sex as you and read the above comments on accountability together. Then read James 5:13–20, paying close attention to verse 16: "Therefore confess your sins to each other and pray for each other so that you may be healed."

Then go off together for a half-hour walk. During that time, tell your partner something you have never told anyone else, and then let your partner pray for you. Then let your partner tell you something, and you pray for him or her.

Does this sound daunting? Sure it does. But I have directed hundreds of men to do this at retreats. They do it. And they come back walking five feet off the ground because they have unloaded something and were accepted anyway. And they each have found a helper who will assist them in the growth into integrity and freedom.

Corporate Responsibility

A few days after the 9/11 tragedy, I was beseeching the Lord for mercy for those who had died. Suddenly it came into my mind to compare the number who had died in those attacks with those who have been killed in the womb in this country. As I did the math, I found that every 18.5 hours for the last thirty years we have aborted as many persons as were killed in the 9/11 attacks. As grieved as we were over those killed in the attacks, our Lord has been at least that grieved once a day for more than thirty years. I think that bears pondering.

At the time of writing this book, the names Enron, WorldCom and Anderson are parading through the headlines with sickening regularity. The stock market has plunged to five-year lows while most other signs of a healthy economy are present. What is wrong? People have realized that persons and companies in corporate groupings have lied to them. The market is suffering. So are investors. One could almost say that the judgment of God is being seen in a market that has placed profit over integrity.

We have excused behaviors in the corporate world that we would never tolerate in the individual. And now it is catching up with us. This is an age-old tendency. But it has never worked. We must face that and apply Jesus' standards of integrity to our corporate identities and relationships.

Some have fallen into a false distinction between the sacred and the secular. Things not tolerated in the sacred realm are accepted in the secular. When that false distinction between the sacred and secular exists, the secular invades the sacred and seeks to convert the sacred to its standards. Look how many leaders in churches have fallen, having been evangelized by the secular realm.

But God is the God of the whole world. There is no sacred and secular distinction for Him, and His standards apply across the board. God declares that dishonesty is wrong whether it is practiced by the individual or the group, whether in church or in the marketplace.

On the positive side, God will surely keep track of and reward every act of integrity in both the church and the world: every act of honesty, every act of courage, every act of kindness, every act of responsibility.

Summing Up

All of our issues have much to do with our relationship with God and with others. For it is relationship—intimacy with us —that Jesus desires:

- It satisfies His longing for us.
- It satisfies our longing for Him.
- It is the empowering factor in doing anything of worth.

By virtue of intimacy with Jesus, He is able to imprint us with His character. Our part is to let Him do it. And letting Him imprint us with His character requires allowing Him to fill us with His Holy Spirit. Please give careful consideration to the teaching notes in Appendix B: About the Baptism with the Holy Spirit.

By the power of the Holy Spirit operating in us, we can grow up in Him, showing His goodness more and more to a world yearning to see Him.

4

The Fifth Command: *Give*

"When I Give through You My Goodness Spreads"

One summer we gave our Sunday school teachers a break by canceling their classes. In place of Sunday school, we modified the church service to be more kid friendly, including brief children's sermons by me. On one of those days as the children were coming up front, I said to the congregation, "The text for this chat is Luke 6:38. For this demonstration, I ask the adults not to speak, but they may act." Then I gathered the children around me and displayed a tray with a three-pound mountain of Jelly Bellies, the Cadillac of jelly beans.

"Would you like a Jelly Belly?" I asked, to which they all nodded vigorously.

So from this mountain, I gave each child one Jelly Belly, which they immediately consumed. Then I waited. Looked at my watch. Gazed around the room. Finally I asked, "Would you like another?"

"*Yes!*" they replied. So I gave them each one more Jelly Belly.

After another pause, this was repeated. But the Jelly Bellies I had distributed had not made any noticeable dent in the huge supply on the tray. I began looking at the adults with a *duh!* kind of look.

Finally, a woman came forward just as I was distributing the fifth Jelly Belly to each child. She approached me holding out her hand for a Jelly Belly. But I said, "I am giving these only to the children." The woman turned to seven-year-old Alicia and vigorously held out her palm, beckoning the child to give away her Jelly Belly.

Alicia looked at the woman, then looked at the lone Jelly Belly in her hand, then back to the woman, then back to her palm, and with a sigh she gave away her Jelly Belly. Immediately I placed two Jelly Bellies in her hand. She gave the lady both of them. I placed four in her hand.

On the next distribution, the children were racing into the congregation to give away their Jelly Bellies and then racing back to me for the double dose. Quickly the children received four, then eight, then sixteen at a dose. Soon there were Jelly Bellies all over the church, and the children were not able to hold all the Jelly Bellies I was putting into their hands.

Give, and It Will Be Given to You

As we reflected on this experience afterward, all present could easily see the truth in Jesus' challenge, "Give, and it will be given to you. A good measure, pressed down, shaken together and running over, will be poured into your lap" (Luke 6:38). We also applauded the woman who read the text and took action on it, for she freed the teaching—as well as the Jelly Bellies—to explode throughout the church.

The command to give—how easily we can receive it as drudgery instead of a blessing! The blessing the children gained from giving away their Jelly Bellies came quickly, but most of the time it takes longer. This leads to another principle: Obedience to Jesus' commands requires the patience to give Him time to act on our obedience and free up the blessings and other results He means to bestow.

The children, of course, had no idea I would give them twice the Jelly Bellies that they gave away. And we adults also have no idea of the blessings the Lord intends to bestow on us because of our obedience in giving. That is where the trust comes in. We have to believe that Jesus loves us better than we love ourselves and that when He tells us to do something, it is for our benefit as well as the benefit of those we are immediately blessing.

Earlier I referred to the story about Jesus speaking to me through Matthew 25 and admonishing me to take in strangers. Obeying this command brought us countless blessings. One blessing that came as a result of our obedience was that it freed Him to give us a three-week trip to Germany, Jordan, the Holy Land and Greece. Another blessing came through a homeless young man who came to my office in the church one day.

He had been living for several months in the hills. Whenever a homeless person came into our office, I always looked at Jesus in my mind's eye and if He nodded, I invited the person into our home. Jesus nodded this time, and the young man accepted the invitation. But he could stand to be under a roof for only three days and then left. While he was with us, however, two of my sons, Kevin and David, came to me one evening.

"Dad," they said, "you know that guy staying with us?"

"Yeah."

"Well, he can't remember anything he said even two minutes before."

As I digested that, I replied, "Hmmm, well, you know he has been a pretty heavy drug user."

Their eyes turned to saucers as they exclaimed, "*That's* what drugs do to you?!"

That was one small, but potentially immense, blessing that came from obeying Jesus' command to take in strangers. I have often said that I would have paid that young man to have that influence on my sons. I could not have foreseen this blessing when I was first wondering whether to take him in or not. But I think Jesus had it in mind.

Was there more that the Lord wanted to do for that young man in our house? I am quite sure there was. But He honored the young man's decision to go back to the hills after three days. He always honors our decisions, even the ones that will not produce the best results for us. He blessed us richly for having taken in the young man, though the young man did not get all that Jesus wanted for *him* in our home.

Why does Jesus want us to give? So He can bless us! As He said, "It is more blessed to give than to receive" (St. Paul quotes Him in Acts 20:35).

One day a man who understood giving came to my office. After I greeted him, he said, "I have two things I want to talk about with you. First, an old college chum is dropping by tonight and he needs inner healing. Will you teach me how to pray for him?"

"Sure," I replied. I got out teaching notes on the subject and went to the heart of them. In twenty minutes he understood the basics of that ministry.

Then he said, "Now for item number two." He reached into his inner coat pocket and extracted an envelope, which he handed to me.

"What's this?" I asked.

"Open it."

I slit the envelope open and took out a check to my church for eighty thousand dollars.

"What's this for?" The words jerked off my lips.

"You tell me," he replied.

"You mean you are giving us eighty thousand dollars with no strings attached?"

"Yes."

Well, that kind of thing drives me to prayer. The next day found me on a trail up in the mountains seeking God for what

He wanted us to do with that money. Finally I heard Him say, *Give half of it away.*

When I told that to our board, they did not think I had heard God correctly. For four months we argued about what to do with that money. Finally the Lord gave us a clue that allowed for agreement and unity. We did indeed give forty thousand dollars to others, some of it in the form of airfare for our teams to go out and minister to other churches.

Less than a year later, this same fellow called me and stated that he needed to make "another delivery." He asked when he might come.

"Whenever you want!" was my reply.

This time the check was for two hundred thousand dollars. I staggered into church and gravitated to the altar, upon which I laid the check.

"Why have You done this?"

I like what you did with the last batch, came the reply.

What a God! What a surprising, generous, clever, wonderful God! We found, indeed, that it is more blessed to give than to receive. Over the next decade, in fact, we gave away about a third of a million dollars in ministries to the wider Church, not to mention cash amounts that averaged about 30 percent of our income. This from a congregation that normally had only about 170 people in church on Sundays! And the man who donated the $280,000? His personal life bore many signs of blessing. His testimony is that he is glad he gave.

But our giving not only blesses us. It also, of course, blesses the recipients. Our giving enables others to get what they need. It lightens their loads. It helps others to see the hand of God at work for them and enables them to minister to others. It helps them to enjoy life more. If I stacked all the letters of thanks we received, the pile would exceed six inches in depth. Each of them reports blessings from the Lord given through us. And that leads me to the next section.

What Does Jesus Want Us to Give?

The most quoted verse in the Bible is about giving: "For God so loved the world that he gave his one and only Son, that whoever believes in him shall not perish but have eternal life" (John 3:16). God gave away the thing that was most precious to Him.

If we are going to be like Him, we must address the question: What does Jesus want us to give away? The expendables are time, energy and money. They are worth something. So He wants us to give what is valuable. Ah, but what is valuable can be difficult to part with!

Consider the following quotes:

- "Withhold thy gift from the poor until he deserveth it."
- "Withhold thy tithe from the church until thou has agreed on the path it hath taken."
- "Withhold thy tithe from the church until it has a concern worth investing in."
- "Withhold thy tithe from the church until thou canst afford to."
- "Give not to him whose need is not proven."
- "The word *tithe* really meaneth not 10 percent but whatever thou feelest like giving."

These are not Scripture verses, of course. But it seems more people obey these "verses" than follow the instructions the Bible offers on giving.

Greed

Jesus apparently discerned some greed in the heart of the fellow who asked Him to make his brother divide the inheritance with him, for Jesus said to the disciples, "Watch out! Be on your guard against all kinds of greed" (Luke 12:15). We can be greedy for all kinds of things: status, money, power, possessions.

Following this admonition Jesus told the parable of the rich fool. The punch line is verse 21: "This is how it will be with anyone who stores up things for himself but is not rich toward God." "Stores up" in Greek is *thesaurizoon* from which we get *thesaurus*. It is also translated as "treasure" or "strongbox."

Jesus ridicules the farmer who makes bigger barns to store up his harvest. He calls him a fool and asks that enlightening question at the end of his life: "Then who will get what you have prepared for yourself?"

Greed is distrust of God. Both the rich and the poor can suffer from it. The rich keep amassing more wealth, and the poor worry about their lives. Both distrust God. Jesus indicates that the proper course is to be "rich toward God." How do we do that? The only way we can be generous to *God* is to bless other *people* with our gifts. Mammon itself does not endure, but it may be used to achieve something that does endure. "Store up for yourselves treasures in heaven," Jesus exhorted (Matthew 6:20). By giving to meet others' needs we bank eternal benefits, and we oppose the spirit of greed.

You see, greed is not just gauche. Greed is much more than stinginess toward God and others. It is a major disqualifier from the eternal Kingdom of God. "For of this you can be sure: No immoral, impure or *greedy person*—such a man is an idolater—has any inheritance in the kingdom of Christ and of God" (Ephesians 5:5).

At the time of your death, not only will your amassed possessions be given to someone else, but also you yourself may be disqualified from entering the Kingdom of God. "What good will it be for a man if he gains the whole world, yet forfeits his soul?" Jesus asked (Matthew 16:26). And in 1 Corinthians 6:9–10, St. Paul concurs: "Neither . . . thieves nor the greedy nor drunkards nor slanderers nor swindlers will inherit the kingdom of God."

"You cannot serve both God and Money!" Jesus exclaimed (Matthew 6:24). At issue is the godliness of God. Who is your

God? Is God your God, or is money your god? "Put to death . . . greed, which is idolatry" (Colossians 3:5). Greed says, "God is not God." Greed says, "That for which I am greedy is my god." Greed disobeys the very first Commandment: "You shall have no other gods before me" (Exodus 20:3). Greed, therefore, is enmity with God.

Greed can express itself today in a variety of ways:

- A believer might say, "I am going to get my needs met!" *But only God can adequately meet your needs.*
- Fidelity Funds might tell you, "You need to store up about $1,500,000 to take care of your retirement." *But the parable of the rich fool settled that.*
- A shopper says, "I will be totally happy as soon as I get my new computer/outfit/car/house." *No, you will not. Only God can satisfy the human heart.*
- Advertisements all over the place tell you, "You can have it all!" *Yes, you can, but not that way.*
- Many of us think, "My friends will think well of me when I own fine things." *But Jesus tells us that a man's life does not consist in the abundance of his possessions.*

Here I offer some advice that will help you in dealing with money and controlling greed. I have found these principles to be invaluable in my life:

1. Stay out of debt. This frees God to mature you.
2. Make the decision to trust God for your needs. This frees God to prove His provision.
3. Rebuke greed. This frees God to give you financial discernment.
4. Value God over everything else. This frees God to change your heart.
5. Cultivate generosity. This frees God to store up treasure for you in heaven.

Generosity

God says,

> "Will a man rob God? Yet you rob me. But you ask, 'How do we rob you?' In tithes and offerings. You are under a curse—the whole nation of you—because you are robbing me. Bring the whole tithe into the storehouse, that there may be food in my house. Test me in this," says the LORD Almighty, "and see if I will not throw open the floodgates of heaven and pour out so much blessing that you will not have room enough for it. I will prevent pests from devouring your crops, and the vines in your fields will not cast their fruit," says the LORD Almighty.

Malachi 3:8–11

Early in this chapter we looked at Luke 6:38: "Give, and it will be given to you. A good measure, pressed down, shaken together and running over, will be poured into your lap. For with the measure you use, it will be measured to you." This is Jesus' version of the Malachi passage. Notice that Jesus does not stipulate the percentage of the gift. But He does correlate the amount of the return with the amount of the investment.

Like all expressions of obedience, tithing is not a legalistic transaction but a matter of the heart. How much to tithe and what money should be tithed are issues greatly debated among the Church, and yet it all boils down to where our hearts are focused: "For where your treasure is, there your heart will be also" (Matthew 6:21). The question: How is your heart in relation to God? The clue: Look in your checkbook.

Our objections are many:

- "I cannot afford to tithe." *The truth is: You cannot afford not to tithe.*
- "I will tithe when I get a job." *Holding out on God moves Him to hold out on your job prospects. Of all times to trust God, now is that time!*

- "I make too much to tithe." *Well, God can reduce your income to the point where you can afford to tithe.*
- "Tithing seems legalistic to me." *Only those who want to give less than 10 percent consider a tithe legalistic. You are arguing with God, not man.*
- "I will tithe when I catch up." *You are kidding yourself. The only way you are going to get caught up is to start trusting God now.*

What is the personal issue at stake in considering a tithe? It is trust in God. It is commitment to *Him* before *everything* else.

Do you trust God to care for you? Do you trust that He will do what He says He will do? If so, the blessing He promises is too great to ignore.

> "Test me in this," says the LORD Almighty, "and see if I will not throw open the floodgates of heaven and pour out so much blessing that you will not have room enough for it. I will prevent pests from devouring your crops, and the vines in your fields will not cast their fruit," says the LORD Almighty.
>
> Malachi 3:10–11

What Does This Mean to Us Today?

Floodgates means blessing will come. *Pests* are unforeseen financial setbacks that will be kept away from you. *Cast fruit* means your plans will not go screwy but will prove to be profitable.

My testimony is that you cannot pay me not to tithe. Before I began to tithe, I was a religious dabbler. It was 1973 and I had been filled with the Spirit the year before, so I was changing. Then God offered me a double challenge: Get out of debt and begin tithing. This seemed crazy. We owned no house. We had three kids (and a fourth arrived two years later). Our financial affairs were in a mess—credit cards maxed out, expensive habits and tastes.

But we cut up all the credit cards, as I mentioned previously. And when I figured out how much we were giving at that time, it was about 3.5 percent. I just did not have the courage to go all the way up to 10 percent, so I split the difference and gave about 7 percent for the remaining six months of that year.

But God swung into action to bless us. Almost imperceptibly, our tastes changed. We no longer felt deprived if we did not go out to dinner regularly. We suddenly got wisdom concerning purchases we had to make. We started receiving more money.

Then, test time! Our refrigerator began making noises. The repairman said the disease was terminal. The temptation was to go out and buy a new one right away, but the Lord had said to get *out* of debt, not get into more. So Sue made a bank out of a coffee can, decorating it with a label that said "Icea-Boxa-Banka." Whenever we had any extra money, we put it in there. Meanwhile, we laid hands on the fridge and prayed that it would last long enough.

Three months later the noises became more urgent. I had researched new refrigerators and had determined that the largest side-by-side made by G.E. was what we needed. When we opened the Icea-Boxa-Banka, we went out and paid cash for a $680 fridge. CASH! C-A-S-H! We had not paid cash for anything more expensive than shoes for the kids.

When the next year began, we declared that we were going to pay the full 10 percent to the Lord and do it gladly. In the subsequent thirty years of tithing, we have learned several things.

1. We have learned how to trust God in very practical matters. Time and again He has proved His faithfulness.
2. We have learned that you cannot out-give God. The more we give Him, the more He gives us back.
3. We have found that *we* are blessed by our generosity more than anyone else. Our hearts have changed. We do not give to get; we give to get to give. The final goal has to be

giving rather than getting. It is indeed more blessed to give, for a giving heart is ever so much more fun to have than a getting one.

4. We have learned how capable He is of using the money we give Him for the extending of His Kingdom.

5. We have learned that when people tithe to the ministries we lead, God swings into action to make those ministries worthy of the people's support. We have been changed, pruned and anointed because of the tithes of others.

6. We have learned that when you lose your life for His sake, you find your life. And our money is a significant part of our lives. More than half of Jesus' parables are about money.

7. We have learned that God is a better money manager than we are. We spend very little time or energy managing our finances—we just tithe, and He seems to handle most of the rest.

8. We have received things we never could have received if we had hoarded that 10 percent for ourselves. I like to travel, for example. At last count, we have visited 44 foreign countries and 49 states. And often we have traveled at someone else's expense. God has just showered us with these wonderful opportunities to travel.

9. We have learned that even in thin times, we should tithe as an act of faith. I challenged all the out-of-work people in my last congregation to tithe on whatever money they did have—unemployment checks or welfare or gifts—and within six weeks all of them had better jobs than they had lost.

10. Finally, we have realized that we are storing up for eternal life. Remember, if eternity is only a million years long, it will be 12,500 times longer than the life of a person who dies at eighty. Think of all the treasure in heaven we are going to enjoy! And think of *how long* we are going to enjoy it.

My advice is that you tithe on every bit of money that comes into your house. Tithing is an act of giving, and giving is the fifth commandment Jesus gives us. It allows His goodness to spread through us. Tithing is an act of faith, a way we show our trust in God, and it releases God to do what He wants to do in our lives and the lives of others.

And one final note about tithing: There is a difference between tithes and alms. Alms go beyond the tithe. As the tithe went into the Temple treasury and alms went to needs beyond the Temple, so our tithe should go to the general fund of the church and our alms—our gifts above and beyond the 10 percent—can go to special needs to which our hearts feel led.

Give Ministry: Words *and* Works

When Jesus said, "Follow me" (Matthew 4:19; 8:22; 9:9; 10:38; 16:24; 19:21; Mark 1:17; 2:14; 8:34; 10:21; Luke 5:27; 9:23, 59; 14:27; 18:22; John 1:43; 10:27; 12:26; 21:19, 22), He set an agenda for believers that only He Himself can fulfill. Yet that agenda calls forth specific attitudes and behaviors on our part. He alone can build the house, yet He chooses to build it through us. "Follow Me," He says, into character, into relationship, into service, into mission, into ministry, into leadership and into understanding. And He provides us a model for how to follow Him: His own record of following the Father.

As my mentor, John Wimber, used to say: The ministry of Jesus manifested an oscillation between saying the *words* of the Kingdom and doing the *works* of the Kingdom. The works verified the words, and the words explained the works. They were a unity, flip sides of one coin.

Right after the Sermon on the Mount, for instance—which is all about the Kingdom—Matthew says,

When he came down from the mountainside, large crowds followed him. A man with leprosy came and knelt before him and said, "Lord, if you are willing, you can make me clean."

Jesus reached out his hand and touched the man. "I am willing," he said. "Be clean!" Immediately he was cured of his leprosy.

Matthew 8:1–3

Jesus' sermon was words; His healing of the leper was works.

If you look at the summaries of Jesus' ministry in the gospels, they nearly always focus on words *and* works. For example: "Jesus went throughout Galilee, teaching in their synagogues, preaching the good news of the kingdom, and healing every disease and sickness among the people" (Matthew 4:23).

St. Paul maintained that pattern of words and works. In 1 Corinthians 2, he says he played down the words in order that the demonstration of the Spirit's power would be more obvious, "so that your faith might not rest on men's wisdom, but on God's power" (verse 5).

Part of the reason for the Church's anemia is that we have focused exclusively on saying the words with scant attention to doing the works. Fear, ignorance, self-preservation and misunderstanding the Lord's vision for His Church all have contributed to this avoidance of the works. The Lord, however, is restoring His ministry to the Church. He is teaching us how to do both the words and the works.

This is a bit daunting to most of us. We shrink from attempting to do His works—at least the supernatural ones—for a variety of reasons. First, we have not seen a model of healing at work with which we can identify. God bless the television evangelists who stage crusadelike gatherings in huge auditoriums, but I could do what they do neither for love nor money. I need a style that looks far more "normal" both to me and to the people to whom I am ministering. How about you?

Second, we have not been exposed to a theology that includes healing in the modern age. This may require some reading, listening to experienced teachers and observation of current ministries.

And third, we have not been taught how to minister to those in need. I have done over 350 conferences all over the United States and Pacific Rim in which people have been healed and taught how to heal. It is not hard to find groups that are effectively ministering to the sick. Maybe a go-and-see expedition is necessary for those who need to be taught how to minister in this way.

When I do conferences, each teaching is followed by a clinic—a hands-on opportunity to see ministry modeled, to try it oneself and to be available for the Spirit to give an impartation for ongoing ministry. A major goal of these conferences is to get the ministry out of the pulpit and into the pew, where it belongs.

Another goal is to model vulnerability to the Lord as normative for life and ministry. The usual result is that many people catch a new vision of what is possible, are healed, are taught, are anointed and are experienced and encouraged in ministry. The Holy Spirit loves to back up those who make themselves vulnerable to Him.

Some months ago I was doing a retreat for a church board in Michigan. After teaching, I invited the Holy Spirit to descend on the group. All but one person said they could feel the Spirit on them. One man felt he had hot hands, so I asked the Lord to anoint him for healing. As we left for lunch, one woman asked if I would pray for her shoulder, which had arthritis. I grabbed the fellow with the hot hands, and we prayed for her for about ninety seconds. She was healed. It was easy! On that day, this man was taught how to minister, was anointed, became excited about doing ministry and began to walk in his anointing that very day.

Later I invited the Holy Spirit down on the group again. At the end of the weekend, the majority of the members explicitly testified that it was the most valuable retreat they had ever attended. But I do not think the teachings were so great that weekend. You understand? It was just the *combination* of the words and works of Jesus.

The words and the works are meant to be the norm, not the exception, to the activities of the people of God. One dear lady said she had never felt the presence of God before. It made me weep. We must get over our discomforts and invite and allow God's presence to be a tangible reality in our churches.

The Church is meant to be an army, not an audience—participants, not observers. What does that mean?

Army	Audience
Everybody has a job	Only a few have jobs
Everybody gets trained for their jobs	Few get trained
Each serves a bigger goal	No goals except to be entertained
Each has a right to orders	No orders are needed
Each has a commanding officer	No officers are needed
Each belongs to a tight-knit unit	Each is alone or haphazard in group membership
Each learns to fight	Few learn to fight

Healing may be the most important way to minister to others. Seventy-seven percent of the work of Jesus was healing the sick. The other 23 percent was nature miracles, such as multiplying food and stilling storms and stuff like that. In addition, 19.2 percent of the verses in the gospels are about the healing of physical and mental illness and the resurrection of the dead. Healing was then and is now the mainstay of Jesus' works. It is one of the most effective ways to transition from being in the audience to being in the army.

As the Body of Christ, it is vital that we learn to minister and then begin to operate in ministry. We ought to be serving as witnesses of Christ that He is not just about words but works as well.

Other Works: Ministering to the Poor

Ministering to the poor is very, very close to the heart of Jesus. In fact, He identifies *Himself* with the poor to whom we minister:

> For I was hungry and you gave me something to eat, I was thirsty and you gave me something to drink, I was a stranger and you invited me in, I needed clothes and you clothed me, I was sick and you looked after me, I was in prison and you came to visit me.
>
> Matthew 25:35–36

Jesus commands us to minister to the poor. And He backs up the command with a very great threat:

> Depart from me, you who are cursed, into the eternal fire prepared for the devil and his angels. For I was hungry and you gave me nothing to eat, I was thirsty and you gave me nothing to drink, I was a stranger and you did not invite me in, I needed clothes and you did not clothe me, I was sick and in prison and you did not look after me.
>
> Matthew 25:41–43

Excuse my bluntness, but the summary of this Scripture is simply: *Help the poor or go to hell.*

Jesus mentions six categories of human need to which He wants us to minister. For the sake of the well-being of the needy and your eternal destiny, it is crucial that you answer the question: How am I doing in ministry to the poor? Whatever aid you give to the Salvation Army is fine, but my advice is that you look for ways to be *personally* involved in helping the poor. Join a program that visits prisoners; serve tables for organizations that feed the hungry; learn how to take in street people and minister effectively and safely to them;[1] organize and/or work at your church's clothing closet and food distribution programs;

visit the sick; or simply give water to the thirsty. If you just send money, you never get to see Jesus' face, but if you minister to the poor in person, you will see His face in theirs.

Every time you obey Jesus, you free Him to plan blessings for you in this life and in the life to come. There *will* be reward—and punishment. God counts and weighs every single act of obedience to Him—even a smile at a homeless person. Remember the ratio of 1 to 12,500? On that proportion, don't you think it will please God and you for you to be rewarded 34.2 *years* in heaven for every *day* that you housed a homeless person? It is foolishness to put such figures down—since eternity is *eternal*—but they are indicative of the vastness of the blessings God means to bestow on you—if you let Him. Obedience is what lets Him.

Other Works: Making Disciples

Making disciples is another work of giving. The Great Commission can be shortened to this: Invest in others. Jesus modeled seven behaviors in His ministry of making disciples, and you can do at least one of them for other persons.[2]

Behavior	Focus
1. He prayed for them.	Selection, protection, unity
2. He recruited them.	Calling
3. He hung out with them.	Friendship
4. He taught them.	Reality, boundary definition (Kingdom)
5. He apprenticed them.	Skill development
6. He debriefed them.	Character development, skill enhancement
7. He anointed them.	Spiritual empowerment

Investing in others has both temporal and eternal benefits. I personally have been the recipient of the investment of several persons who have discipled me in my career. In addition to the reward they will receive for their investments in me, each of them will get some reward for the thousands of people I have taught, healed, trained, encouraged and inspired. And now I receive constant reports from those people on how *they* are teaching, healing, training, encouraging and inspiring others. You cannot imagine what a joy it is to read those reports. In other words, several generations of blessed ones will free the Lord to pile on blessings in the afterlife for those who invested in me.

Other Works: Missions

Toward the end of His earthly time with the disciples, Jesus said, "As the Father has sent me, I am sending you" (John 20:21). A missionary is one who is sent, whether on a short- or long-term mission.

At present count, more than two thousand persons have paid their own way to go with me to pour out blessings on others. Many of those trips have been on weekends, and some of them have been weeks in duration. We have ministered in thirty states and a dozen countries. So I have had the opportunity to observe these short-term missionaries up close. You know what? They thrive on it.

I remember the glee of my team in Argentina as they reported on miracles God did through them.

I think of Cathy carefully interviewing and praying for a woman in the Philippines. That woman's knee was healed under Cathy's hands, which was a first for Cathy. She was jazzed for weeks.

I recall John being challenged in Australia to teach and minister to seven hundred people. He gulped, but he did it. You should have seen the confidence rise in him as he saw people being ministered to under his direction. He then blazed a trail of renewal back and forth across that land.

I think of Lloyd in Los Angeles, who had just forty minutes to instruct and pray for about thirty people to be filled with the Holy Spirit. They were filled and knew it. And Lloyd was deeply satisfied. Then he did it several more times in different places.

I like people to discover what I call "on-the-road anointing." Because of the intensity of the events our ministry hosts, everything—including God's anointing on those traveling with us—intensifies. In a single weekend they may grow the equivalent of months of normal at-home growth. This does wonderful things for their self-image, confidence, relationships and usefulness to the Kingdom. There is benefit all the way around—to them, to those to whom they minister and to the Lord.

There are also long-term missionaries. These are people who have heard the Lord invite them to lay down large segments of their lives in order to minister extensively to those who do not know Jesus. When you give to these people, you are satisfying the yearning in God's heart for those who do not know Him, for it is the nature of Love to seek more and more beloveds.

Sue and I get deep satisfaction from supporting missionaries. We also spend considerable time, energy and money training missionaries in knowledge and skills they need on the mission field. It is greatly worth that expenditure. The bottom line is that those missionaries are freed to fulfill God's call on their lives.

The Seven Steps of Collaboration with Jesus

In the story of the feeding of the five thousand, we see the steps that it takes to collaborate effectively with God in the act of giving, whether the need requires a natural or supernatural answer:

> As evening approached, the disciples came to him and said, "This is a remote place, and it is already getting late. Send the crowds away, so they can go to the villages and buy themselves some food."
>
> Jesus replied, "They do not need to go away. You give them something to eat."

"We have here only five loaves of bread and two fish," they answered.

"Bring them here to me," he said. And he directed the people to sit down on the grass. Taking the five loaves and the two fish and looking up to heaven, he gave thanks and broke the loaves. Then he gave them to the disciples, and the disciples gave them to the people. They all ate and were satisfied, and the disciples picked up twelve basketfuls of broken pieces that were left over. The number of those who ate was about five thousand men, besides women and children.

Matthew 14:15–21

And from John's version of this episode:

"Gather the pieces that are left over. Let nothing be wasted." So they gathered them and filled twelve baskets with the pieces of the five barley loaves left over by those who had eaten.

John 6:12–13

All right, what are the steps involved in this collaboration of man and God?

1. *We are to do it!* "You give them something to eat" (Matthew 14:16). This probably takes the breath away, for often the need is way beyond our ability to meet it. Our immediate response, like the disciples, is to quickly tally up our inability to meet the need. But there is the naked command: "You do it!"

2. *We bring Him our inadequate resources.* "We have here only five loaves of bread and two fish" (verse 17). Bring whatever resources you do have—however lacking—to Him. Put yourself at His feet, along with your feeble amounts of time, energy, money and skill.

3. *He makes them adequate.* "'Bring them here to me.' . . . Taking the five loaves and the two fish and looking up to heaven, he gave thanks and broke the loaves" (verse 18). *How* does He make these piddling offerings adequate? I do not know. But He has done it time and time again. He will do it for you, too.

4. *He gives them back to us.* "Then he gave them to the disciples" (verse 19). Almost as soon as you put your resources at His disposal, He gives them back with the notion that you are to use them. They do not look any different yet.

5. *We give them to others.* "And the disciples gave them to the people" (verse 19). Start the program! Begin to act! Launch out! Get going!

6. *His adequacy is revealed as we act.* "They all ate and were satisfied" (verse 20). Somehow, working through you, He makes the thing work. I am pretty sure each disciple walked into the crowd with one-twelfth of five muffins and two sardines—not much! The miracle of multiplication happened *as they gave* these pieces to the people.

7. *Do not waste what He has made available.* "'Gather the pieces that are left over. Let nothing be wasted.' So they gathered them and filled twelve baskets with the pieces of the five barley loaves left over by those who had eaten" (John 6:12–13). Let nothing go to waste—not results, not learnings, not praise to God, not the satisfaction of having been used by the living God.

Now, I began by saying that these steps work whether the need can be met by natural or supernatural means. Some things look less supernatural than others, such as organizing a youth retreat to the mountains. But my advice is that you regard anything you think God wants you to do as beyond your ability. That brings Jesus into active collaboration with you. Then go through the seven steps.

Put yourself in the disciples' shoes. Don't you think they were awed, excited and united by their experience in that feeding episode? Don't you think they told that story over and over to their families and friends? You bet they did. God wants to give you stories just like that.

Giving Acts of Love

Sometimes the thing we are to give is from largeness of heart. Jesus can tell us to do some things that are clearly beyond the requirements of justice, politeness or normal expectations. These are little acts of grace, the Sermon on the Mount kinds of things: "If someone strikes you on the right cheek, turn to him the other also. And if someone wants to sue you and take your tunic, let him have your cloak as well. If someone forces you to go one mile, go with him two miles" (Matthew 5:39–41). *Strike, sue* and *force* are aggressive words. But Jesus is saying to accept the aggression and sap it of its strength by doubling its own demands.

How many acts of grace, sometimes called "Chicken Soup" stories, have you heard that touched your heart? Often it is this second-mile dynamic that touches us. Grace is unexpected. And when it shows up, it is enormously powerful. Almost always, God strategizes so that grace occurs through the collaboration of people like you. A quick act of grace can change literally a whole life in a matter of seconds.

One such act of grace happened to me in December of 1979. I first noticed it during the Communion service one Thursday but could not tell what it was. After the service I went to the ledge that held flowers on Sundays to find a note on a somewhat used three-by-five-inch piece of paper. On top of it were a worn black, plastic cross and medallion with five beads between them on a string. This is what the note looked like, in the handwriting of maybe a nine-year-old girl:

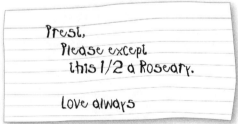

Prest,
Please except
this 1/2 a Roseary.

Love always

On the back of the note was the number "2000" in the five places that such a figure would be printed on a monetary bill. Sitting down at my desk, I was simply swept with the honor of receiving such a gift. Waves of warmth coursed through me as

I realized that some child had stolen into an empty church—sometimes a formidable thing to do—to leave her version of two thousand dollars' worth of love in a note and a rosary.

Isn't two thousand just about infinity to a child? I thought. The spelling of *priest, accept* and *rosary* made it all the more charming. The love of Jesus filled my heart as softly as the caress of a feather on one's cheek.

As I wondered who this child was who had so captivated my adoration, it was as though the Lord said to me, *It was I. You have ministered to a few people not knowing that they were I. So now you have been ministered to by a little girl who was I.*

I have never forgotten this act of grace. It changed me. I still have the "roseary" and the note. And each time I remember it, it makes me cast through my mind for someone on whom I might make such a sneak attack of love. With those thoughts comes a kind of gleeful innocence that bubbles up in me as I anticipate the joy of sneaking up on someone to deposit a load of love.

"Give, and it will be given to you. A good measure, pressed down, shaken together and running over, will be poured into your lap" (Luke 6:38). The command to give is meant not only to bless others but also to bless those of us who give. When we obey Jesus' command to give, we invite the blessings and other results He wants to bestow on us. And as we give, Jesus' goodness spreads through us.

5

The Fourth Command: *Watch*

"I Want to Be Alert in You"

J esus' fourth strongest command is to watch, or watch out. This can be a dangerous world, and we have a dangerous enemy. As Jesus was preparing to finish His work on the earth and go back to heaven, He emphasized the need to be on the lookout. Most of His warnings about watching, therefore, came in the eschatological discourses or end-times teachings He gave. In a single chapter, Mark 13, He urged us to watch out five times. He told numerous parables with the same point. In the book of 2 John, verse 8 echoes the point: "Watch out that you do not lose what you have worked for, but that you may be rewarded fully." This verse indicates that not to watch might be to lose one's reward.

What things does Jesus think we should watch out for? Without making the list too exhaustive, we can list seven warnings.

1. Watch Out for Deception

"Watch out that no one deceives you" (Matthew 24:4; Mark 13:5; Luke 21:8). Deception begins when some problem presents itself, suggests a quite reasonable but unbiblical solution and is accepted by a growing number of people who have failed to act on biblical ideas. Deception aims at the mind because the mind contains our ideas of truth and falseness. Any firmly held idea gives rise to attitudes, evaluations, priorities and behaviors. If the idea is true, that is great. But a firmly held belief in an untruth can cause discord, confusion and calamity.

St. Paul talked about the mind: "We demolish arguments and every pretension that sets itself up against the knowledge of God, and we take captive every *thought* to make it obedient to Christ" (2 Corinthians 10:5). "But I am afraid that just as Eve was deceived by the serpent's cunning, your *minds* may somehow be led astray from your sincere and pure devotion to Christ" (11:3). And he says, "For although they knew God, they neither glorified him as God nor gave thanks to him, but their *thinking* became futile and their foolish hearts were darkened" (Romans 1:21). Paul's argument is that the mind is one of Satan's targets. Someone pointed out that the battle for the mind is the task of every generation.

Almost every magazine contains the results of some new study whose conclusions sound credible. But wait six months and those conclusions are superseded by yet another article. And, unfortunately, such roller-coaster dynamics of truth-then-untruth are not restricted to the unbelieving world. Anyone can find plenty of evidence of argument over what is true in a single aisle of a Christian bookstore. What is a Christian to do?

Our job is to pull down ideas, philosophies and systems of thought that conflict with God's. My advice is to go back to Jesus. Scripture that is read and acted upon is the surest safeguard against deception.

I cannot emphasize enough the importance of reading the Scriptures. Only in this way can the holy words of God pierce our hearts and transform our lives, safeguarding us against deception. Recognizing the immense value of reading and acting upon Scripture, let me pause here to offer a bit of advice. If you read one chapter of the gospels each day, you will read all of them four times a year and have nine days left over. I have been doing this for 25 years. Many things that I needed to see in the gospels I did not see until I had read them a number of times. This reading plan provides for that number of times. Besides, on this plan you encounter the crucifixion sixteen times a year. That keeps you close to the central reality of why the Father sent the Son. And being in the Word daily in this way helps to protect us from deceptive teachings.

A young mother who had been raised in a cult came to my office one day. Even though her religion spoke glowingly of Jesus, she was confused. For a while, I did not know how to help her, for every time I mentioned a biblical truth about Jesus, she countered with an opposing statement from her religion.

"I would like to believe you," she said, "but I do not know whether you are deceived or not." *Fair enough,* I thought. So I prayed, saying in my mind something really sophisticated such as, "Help!" The Lord did help me. He put into my mind a challenge, which I simply relayed to her: "Will the real Jesus please stand up?" I advised her to pray that prayer daily for a month and then see what happened. In addition, I urged her to read a chapter of the gospels each day, asking the Lord to open her mind to what it said.

A month later she returned.

"Okay," she said, "He stood up. And now I have to leave that religion. What do I do now?" As I interviewed her, it became clear that Jesus had indeed revealed Himself to this woman. She now knew the difference between the real Jesus and the one her religion had promoted.

Since then, I have issued that same challenge to believing Christians who were propounding ideas about Jesus that irritated my spirit. If they were sincere about finding the truth, they usually found it by going straight to Jesus and asking Him to clarify.

What I am talking about here is the gift of discernment. It is an enabling by the Holy Spirit that points us to the truth about something. It works in tight unity with the Scriptures and allows the Scriptures to teach us the full truth.

What I am going to say now may seem simplistic, but hang in there with me for a minute. I figure God is clever enough to know the truth, have it written in a Book, require that faith is what it takes to read and understand the Book, give us that faith and direct us all through our lives as we read that Book.

Let's break that statement apart step-by-step. First, will you assume with me that God is true and knows the full dimensions of all truth at every level? That is, He cannot be deceived.

Will you also assume that He is wise and subtle and clever enough to inspire human beings to write down His Word? And will you believe that He managed to get sufficient agreement among followers about what writings are and are not to be included in His Book?

Next—and this is really important—let's assume that He decided, as He says in His Book, that it takes faith in Him for someone to comprehend His Book. The Bearer of this faith is His Holy Spirit. "The man without the Spirit does not accept the things that come from the Spirit of God, for they are foolishness to him, and he cannot understand them, because they are spiritually discerned" (1 Corinthians 2:14). So faith from the Holy Spirit begins to reveal the truth of Scripture for us.

Let's also assume that He gives us this faith if we ask for it. As we read His Book we give Him access to our Spirit-enabled minds to see and act on His directions.

Now, there is a bit of a hitch, and it runs contrary to the way we like things to work. The hitch is this, and it is another of our principles: Often we cannot understand *why* God tells us to do something in His Word until *after* we have taken action in obedience to it.

What that means, of course, is that we cannot remain neutral about God or His Word when we are deciding whether or not to believe it. Obedience is commitment. Obedience puts us over the line of wondering whether the thing is true or not. "There is no authority without submission. . . . In order to be joined to Jesus and have His authority, we must be His obedient servants."[1]

In *The Mustard Seed Book* I spent much time elaborating on this dynamic.[2] The bottom line is that obedience precedes understanding, and obedience precedes emotional integration. But as long as we insist that something biblical makes sense to our intellects before we take action on it, we are deceived.

Let me elaborate on a story I mentioned in chapter 2. You remember that I was reading along in the Bible one day when the words "I was a stranger and you took me in" jumped off the page into my mind. Well, as I said, I did not want to take in street people so pretended that I did not see those words. But after talking with Sue, I knew God had showed me that passage for a reason, so we took in the boy.

A week after this young man came into our home, he was walking through the room where I was sitting, and I glanced at him. Suddenly it was as though I had had tight blinds over my eyes and they snapped open to reveal that this boy was Jesus Christ "in His distressing disguise," as Mother Teresa calls the poor. I thought, *If I want to minister to Jesus Christ, here He is, close at hand, in my own home.* That boy lived with us over a year. He was the first of scores of homeless people God brought into our home.

Now here's the point again: Until I obeyed that underlined injunction in the Word, confirmed by the social worker's request, I could not understand *why* God wanted me to take in strangers. But having acted, my eyes were opened—and so was my heart.

Do not wait to obey until you understand. Obey what you think the Lord is telling you to do and then expect understanding—and much more—to follow. One of my favorite writers is

George MacDonald. He stated it this way: "Men would understand; they do not care to obey. They try to understand where it is impossible they should understand except by obeying. They would search into the work of the Lord instead of doing their part in it. . . . It is on them that do His will that the day dawns. To them the daystar arises in their hearts. Obedience is the soul of knowledge."[3]

"Are you saying that *nothing* in Scripture can be understood without prior obedience?" someone might ask. No, I am not. Reality is too complex for that. But there are levels of understanding. In the story I told above, I understood that Jesus was saying *Take in a stranger* before I did it. And I could see that doing so would provide a roof and a bed and food for this person. And I could even have generated some compassion for that boy. But it was not until I had acted and he was already under my roof that the full dimensions of Jesus' wishes could be made clear to me. And it was not until I had acted that God could impact my heart at heart level about the homeless.

Even as I write this I know that some readers will be unable to get what I am saying. If God has it in mind for *you* to take in a stranger, you will not be able to do more than give an entry-level assent to the idea until you actually do it. Does this mean that God wants *every* believer to take in strangers? No. Some are simply not in circumstances that would permit that. But do not be too quick to exempt yourself if God seems to point at you to do this.

Let me give you another example. In 1988, I read that my denomination, the Episcopal Church, was having its national convention in Phoenix the following July. Phoenix was not that far from my church in Southern California. Right away I saw an image of myself facedown on the floor of a Phoenix hotel room praying for the Episcopal Church. Well, that convention goes on for ten days, and I was mad at the Episcopal Church, so I immediately said, "No way!" and put it out of my mind.

One month before that convention, I was praying early one Sunday when the Lord brought to mind that picture of myself praying on my face in Phoenix. He said, *Put aside your sermon and tell the congregation about that picture.* I did not *want* to do it, I did not see any *reason* to do it, and when I asked, "Why?" I got no answer.

But I knew I either had to do it because He said so or not do it because I said so. I sighed deeply with resignation. "All right, I will do it, but it seems to be a waste of a good sermon."

So I told the congregation about that picture of myself praying in Phoenix. Then, aha! I said suddenly, "I cannot go to Phoenix for ten days because I do not have the money. And this is *not* an appeal for funds! But if you think I am supposed to go, put something extra in the collection plate."

This was a setup. Someone there had just received an inheritance and tithed five thousand dollars of it for this purpose! When I saw that, I knew I was going—and not by myself. God arranged for fifteen members of my congregation and me to book a number of rooms in a small hotel. The hotel had only two meeting rooms. We reserved one of the conference rooms, and it turned out that the group that promotes homosexual relationships in the Episcopal Church occupied the other. This group was part of the movement in our denomination that was causing my anger and frustration, as the promotion of homosexuality at that time was beginning to cause a real rift among the Episcopal Church—one threatening us even more today.

Remember that I said deception begins when some problem presents itself, suggests a quite reasonable but unbiblical solution and is accepted by a growing number of people who fail to act on biblical ideas. I said that deception aims at the mind, and any firmly held idea gives rise to attitudes, evaluations, priorities and behaviors. And a firmly held belief in an untruth causes discord, confusion and calamity. This is what we are seeing happen in the Episcopal Church and other denominations that are struggling with issues such as this one.

When we began meeting in that hotel, just feet from the gay group, we realized that we had to pray for them. Prior to that, I had been able to sustain a judgmental attitude toward gays and those in the Church who promote their interests. But after several days of praying for them—as well as for the Church at large—God broke our hearts for gay people. We did not change our minds that gay behavior is sin, but we wept for the brokenness that produces gay behavior. We smiled at the homosexuals as we passed them in the halls. We refused to judge them. We pleaded with God to have mercy on them. We entered into spiritual warfare against the tendencies that manipulate them. We begged God to forgive those in the Church who endanger the eternal standing of gays by excusing their behavior.

In other words, we came closer to the attitudes that Jesus promotes about enemies and those who are misled. But that came only after praying for them—which is just what Jesus says to do for those who are opposed to you.

You see, *their* deception was thinking that God could bless homosexual behavior, but *my* deception was thinking that lecturing them about their sin would make a difference. After praying for them, I was changed. I now had a new approach to evaluating and interacting with homosexuals. And several of them have been healed into freedom from that lifestyle.

The point here is that Jesus wants us to always be on guard against deception of any kind. And discernment given by the Holy Spirit—and backed up by Scripture and prayer—is our best means of defense. Finally, often our job is to obey what God tells us to do, even if we do not understand it at the time, for sometimes a full measure of understanding comes only through the doing.

2. Watch for the Second Coming of Jesus

Watching for Jesus' return is the second strongest exhortation under the command to "Watch!" Many of the end-time parables teach us how to behave watchfully and be ready for Him when He comes back. In fact, 33 of Jesus' 38 parables have to do with being included or excluded in eternal life.[4] Do not let Him catch you napping! Our readiness must be demonstrated in a variety of ways.

• *Fruitfulness.* The Lord expects us to be fruitful. This means being at work for His Kingdom. In the parable of the talents, the fellows who were commended—included—were the ones who put their talents to work to produce benefit for the Lord. The one who was rebuked was excluded for laziness.

• *Watchfulness.* Keep alert. Do not get drunk, do not be lazy, do not be wicked—these things will cause you to be excluded. The parable of the five foolish and five wise virgins has to do with readiness by virtue of being full of the Spirit. Oil is usually symbolic of the Spirit in the New Testament. Those who ran out of oil were empty of the Spirit and were therefore not ready when the King came. It takes the Spirit of God to keep you ready for the Son of God's return. I ask the Spirit to fill me daily because I leak.

• *Canniness.* Several of Jesus' warnings regarding His return have to do with not being gullible. He states clearly that everyone will know instantaneously when He comes. He warns that many will claim to be He or will claim that He is here or there. But He says, "Do not be deceived." So believers, who should always be ready to believe and to act, are warned that they should not believe and act on the advice of charlatans. A little godly agnosticism toward claimants will go a long way toward keeping you safe.

• *Endurance.* "Be always on the watch, and pray that you may be able to escape all that is about to happen, and that you may be able to stand before the Son of Man" (Luke 21:36). Jesus clearly predicts that there will be tough times. Some of them will be so tough, in fact, that if there were not a divine shortening of those days, none would make it. The message is, Hang on! Do not give in. Do not lose hope.

• *Reward and Punishment.* Jesus reminds us that there will be reward and punishment. The focus of the Second Coming will be a throne on which Jesus sits to pronounce judgment. There will be division among people. We see a few examples of these divisions in the books of Matthew and Luke:

Punishment	Reward
Matthew 13 no benefit from the seed sown; weeds burned	10, 6 or 3,000 percent return on investment; wheat gathered into barn
Matthew 13 go into the fiery furnace for the wicked	good fish collected into baskets
Matthew 18 unforgiving servant turned over to jailers	(none mentioned)
Matthew 21 Pharisees rejected from heaven	tax collectors and prostitutes repented and entered the Kingdom of heaven
Matthew 21 those invited did not deserve to come	many invited and received
Matthew 25 five foolish virgins rejected	five wise virgins accepted
Matthew 25 worthless servant thrown out into darkness; weeping and gnashing of teeth	faithful servants given charge of much and share their master's happiness
Matthew 25 eternal punishment for those who did not serve the poor	those who helped the poor receive their inheritance; the Kingdom prepared for them
Matthew 25 rich fool did not get to enjoy his hoard	(none mentioned)
Luke 16 rich man suffered in hell	poor Lazarus comforted in heaven
Luke 17 he who exalts himself will be humbled	he who humbles himself will be exalted

3. Watch Out for Pharisees and Herodians

The third category Jesus wants us to watch out for is the group I call the Pharisees and Herodians. In Scripture these two groups commit opposite mistakes: The Pharisees were legalists; the Herodians were licentious. To Pharisees everything was law. To Herodians there were no laws. Unfortunately, both groups are alive and well in the Church and in the world today.

Neither the licentious nor the legalist is Jesus' idea of what a disciple should be. The licentious operates out of his knowledge of evil, the legalist out of his knowledge of good. Both forfeit their innocence and the peace of Jesus. See the sermon in Appendix C for a full explanation.

Pharisees put rules and regulations ahead of God Himself. Jesus denounced the self-righteousness of the theft-less, evil-less, adultery-less Pharisees who fasted and tithed. In fact, He said that a guilt-ridden but honest sinner went to heaven justified instead of the self-righteous Pharisee. Jesus made Himself accessible to the Pharisees throughout the duration of His ministry and never sent them away, but He did not seek them out to combat them. His advice was to "leave them; they are blind guides" (Matthew 15:14).

The Herodians might be likened to modern people who compromise biblical morality—especially regarding sexuality—because they want to do things the Bible forbids. They become self-deceived, managing to convince themselves that their acts are acceptable. If they can get others to agree with them, it makes their position more plausible, which is why Jesus warned us not to be influenced by them.

Jude said it this way, "For certain men whose condemnation was written about long ago have secretly slipped in among you. They are godless men, who change the grace of our God into a license for immorality and deny Jesus Christ our only Sovereign and Lord" (Jude 4). We are to love them, forgive them and pray for them, but we are not to be influenced by them.

To declare myself, I am convinced that some in the Church are setting back the purposes of the Head of the Church, Jesus. I reckon them to be in one camp or the other: the licentious or the legalists. But for me to write, act, feel and plan in postures of criticism toward them leads to death for them and for me. My task is to avoid pharisaism in *Mike Flynn*.

He whom you criticize is lord of your life. He is the one who has your attention, dictates your actions and determines your emotions. "Judge not" does not just pertain to the one you are tempted to judge; it also pertains to you. You cannot judge and remain unscathed. Let me ask you: How much of your agenda these days is determined by those you oppose? Should it not be Jesus who sets the agenda for you?

I have been so angry and frustrated with what has been going on in my denomination. But one day as I fumed over it, the Lord told me, "The institutional Church is not going to heaven." As I pondered that I realized, of course, that buildings and budgets and church rules and titles and structures are not going to be found in heaven. Only the Body of Christ. Only the believers. That refocused my attention on the positive things I could do to build up the Body and extend the influence of the Kingdom of God here on earth.

So what should be our attitude toward those we feel are ruining the Church? I think the counsel of Scripture is to let them alone. Pray for them, confess for them and bless them, as Jesus counseled. But then get on with the business of proclaiming the Kingdom of God to those who do not know Him—heal their sick, forgive their sins, encourage their hope, meet their needs. A fist-sized lightbulb can dispel hundreds of cubic feet of darkness; a dash of salt can season a whole meal. *You are light, you are salt,* the Boss said. *Be light,* and do not fret so much about the darkness. You have got it vastly outnumbered—*if* you let your light shine.

4. Watch Out for Temptation

Jesus urged His followers several times to pray that they would not fall into temptation. Successful temptation, of course, results in sin, and sin breaks fellowship between God and us. God has made provision for sin through the death and resurrection of Jesus. If you have sinned, call out to Him for the forgiveness He promises to give. But be aware that between your sin and God's forgiveness of it, you are in jeopardy: God's protection is gone, His Spirit is silenced and His presence is far away. In other words, you are on your own.

Let me ask you a series of sequential questions.

- What is your big temptation?
- Do you beat up on yourself when you commit that sin?
- Have you gotten to the point where you quickly confess your sins to God and receive forgiveness when you fall into sin?

- Have you confessed that same sin hundreds of times before?
- Have you discovered that God keeps on forgiving you even though you have committed the same sin many, many times?
- In addition to forgiving your sins, has God begun to discipline you over them?
- Has His discipline motivated you to finally break loose from your sin?
- Are you walking in freedom from that big sin, and are you rejoicing that the Lord dealt with you to the point that you gave it up?

Not everyone goes through all these steps. I am one of those who has. And I suspect that many of you are somewhere on this list.

For those who are facing God's discipline, hear these words from Hebrews 12:

> Endure hardship as discipline; God is treating you as sons. For what son is not disciplined by his father? If you are not disciplined (and everyone undergoes discipline), then you are illegitimate children and not true sons. Moreover, we have all had human fathers who disciplined us and we respected them for it. How much more should we submit to the Father of our spirits and live! Our fathers disciplined us for a little while as they thought best; but God disciplines us for our good, that we may share in his holiness. No discipline seems pleasant at the time, but painful. Later on, however, it produces a harvest of righteousness and peace for those who have been trained by it.
>
> verses 7–11

My testimony is that this is wonderfully true. My big temptation was using pornography. Over the years, the Lord helped me with that problem in a variety of ways. He forgave me, He healed me of underlying causes, He empowered me to resist, He gave me accountability partners and He taught me how to control my thoughts. But I still fell into the use of pornography two or three times a year. So He pulled discipline out of His bag. In a period of weeks He allowed me to have two minor fender benders, an extremely painful neck and the loss of a staff person through my own administrative oversight. Immediately after each of these events, I knew in my knower that it was discipline. There was no other explanation that my heart would believe. That did it! That finished my career with pornography. I began to walk in freedom from that big sin and to rejoice that the Lord dealt with me to the point that I gave it up.

So look out for temptations—

- to sin
- to beat up on yourself
- to refuse to confess after so many sins
- to despair of ever getting better
- to grouse when you are being disciplined

5. Watch Out for Greed

I covered greed at length in chapter 2, so I will be succinct here. Greed is not just being self-centered. It is not just being ungenerous.

The Bible calls greed idolatry. Greed is a form of religion in which we worship something other than the true God. Watch out for it!

6. Watch That You Do Not Lead Others to Sin

Jesus made a simple but dramatic statement about those who lead others into sin, especially children: "It would be better for him to have a large millstone hung around his neck and to be drowned in the depths of the sea" (Matthew 18:6). He went on, "Woe to the world because of the things that cause people to sin!" (verse 7).

In Jesus' mind, the consequences of leading others to sin are utterly catastrophic. So be on guard that you do not lead others to sin. And when you can, use influence with others who currently are guilty of that sin—abusers, seducers, tempters, false teachers—and help them out of those serious sins.

7. Watch Out for Worry

Jesus seems to contradict Himself when addressing a particular topic found in both Matthew and Luke. Let's look at Luke's version:

> I tell you, my friends, do not be afraid of those who kill the body and after that can do no more. But I will show you whom you should fear: Fear him who, after the killing of the body, has power to throw you into hell. Yes, I tell you, fear him. Are not five sparrows sold for two pennies? Yet not one of them is forgotten by God. Indeed, the very hairs of your head are all numbered. Don't be afraid; you are worth more than many sparrows.
>
> Luke 12:4–7

The sequence goes: "Don't be afraid . . . fear him . . . yes, fear him . . . don't be afraid." We almost want to ask Jesus to make up His mind.

But we also know that in Matthew Jesus talks again of the little birds:

> Therefore I tell you, do not worry about your life, what you will eat or drink; or about your body, what you will wear. Is not life more important than food, and the body more important than clothes? Look at the birds of the air; they do not sow or reap or store away in barns, and yet your heavenly Father feeds them. Are you not much more valuable than they? Who of you by worrying can add a single hour to his life?

And why do you worry about clothes? See how the lilies of the field grow. They do not labor or spin. Yet I tell you that not even Solomon in all his splendor was dressed like one of these. If that is how God clothes the grass of the field, which is here today and tomorrow is thrown into the fire, will he not much more clothe you, O you of little faith? So do not worry, saying, "What shall we eat?" or "What shall we drink?" or "What shall we wear?" . . . your heavenly Father knows that you need (all these things). But seek first his kingdom and his righteousness, and all these things will be given to you as well. Therefore do not worry about tomorrow, for tomorrow will worry about itself. Each day has enough trouble of its own.

Matthew 6:25–34

The point is really quite simple: With reference to eternal destiny, do fear God; with reference to daily needs, do not be afraid, for God is looking after you.

Worry is fear of the wrong kind. I have lived long enough to give way to fear numerous times. But our gracious God has led me out of my earthly fears. I have been in what is called a faith ministry now for seven years: I have never gone without a full paycheck—except twice when I was being disciplined. God has met all my needs, and I have decided it is foolish to waste energy fretting about needs.

Watching Sets Us Free to Receive Our Reward

So, Jesus commands us to be on the watch for deception, for His coming again, for legalism and license, for temptation, for greed, for leading others into sin and for worry. Doing these things fulfills His fourth strongest command and sets us free to receive both temporal and eternal rewards.

6

The Third Command: *Forgive*

"My Goodness Heals as I Forgive through You"

Maybe it was a dream. It occurred during that half-asleep, half-awake period when the night is over. My memory of it is not anything like a videotape; rather, I remember only a quick series of mental flashes. But I remember vividly what happened.

It was crucifixion day. Almost dark. Jesus' pitiable body was dangling from nails, nearly dead. A fellow was standing right under Him with his hands cupped upward. As I watched, I realized he was filling his hands with the blood that was dripping from Jesus' body. *What is he going to do with it?* I thought. Before I was able to imagine many options, he suddenly reared back with his right hand and threw the blood back in Jesus' face. I was aghast at that insult, that travesty, and I struggled to grasp what it meant. Then the Lord spoke: *But that is what always happens when someone refuses to forgive.*

To refuse to forgive is to insult the sacrifice of Christ. Not to forgive is to render that sacrifice null and void. Not to forgive is to negate the purpose of Jesus' death. The command to forgive is Jesus' third strongest command.

God's Forgiveness

First we must understand the depth of God's forgiveness of us. The Lord does not even allow our forgiven sins to exist in His memory. Isaiah 38:17 says, "In your love you kept me from the pit of destruction; you have put all my sins behind your back." Hebrews 8:12 quotes Jeremiah 31:34 to make the same point: "For I will forgive their wickedness and will remember their sins no more." And Hebrews 10:16–17 says, "'This is the covenant I will make with them after that time,' says the Lord. 'I will put my laws in their hearts, and I will write them on their minds.' Then he adds: 'Their sins and lawless acts I will remember no more.'"

This is God's part of the equation. Yet, as we will see in a moment, this is actually a conditional promise: It is possible for us to fling those forgotten sins before God's throne once again.

Self-Forgiveness

I am old enough to have committed a good many sins, and as a pastor I have heard about lots of others' sins. One of the things I have learned is that we have to forgive ourselves in order to stop sin's negative influence on ourselves and others. I have uttered and heard several objections to self-forgiveness. Let's look at some of them.

- "What I did was not so bad. Others have done a lot worse."

Any sin separates us from God, even a "minor" one. So it makes sense to get rid of it through confession and forgiveness. In addition, there is a Jesus'-eye view of things. Once the Lord showed me that if I held resentment toward someone who had killed one of my children, my resentment would be the plank in my eye and his murder of my child would be the sliver in his. That sounds a bit extreme, I know. The point is that we must deal with our own sin—which is the plank—before trying to deal with anyone else's.

- "What I did is too bad to forgive."

This problem is the opposite of the previous one. Somehow we create a line in our hearts: Sins on this side of the line are forgivable, and sins on the other side are not. But that line is our creation, not God's. Jesus died for *all* sins, including the worst ones that you or anyone else could commit.

Sometimes I misquote 1 John 1:9 on purpose to make a point with my hearers: "If we confess our sins, he is faithful and just and will forgive us our sins and purify us from *most* unrighteousness." *Most?* No, the text really says *all,* does it not? Yet many of us fail to digest that promise and continue to walk in a state of unforgiveness, not fully applying that *all* to our consciences.

But what about the "unforgivable sin" that Jesus mentions? The unforgivable sin is a sin against the Holy Spirit, whose job is to bring us to awareness that we need a Savior, a Forgiver. If you keep stiff-arming the Holy Spirit, your sin is procedurally unforgivable because you have not yet let God forgive you. But it is not categorically unforgivable.

- "But I have repented of this so many times before."

Here is another line in our hearts that we create but that God does not. This time the line forms through sheer repetition. When we draw this line we are creating a limit and then imposing that limit on God. Instead, we must

105

just confess it again and start over again. Our God is the God of fresh starts. He has more fresh starts than you have sins.

Alan Paton, a South African writer and warden of a reformatory, wrote the following poem as part of a meditation for his son's confirmation in the Church. Can you hear the heart of God for you in it?

> If you should fall into sin, innocent one, that is the way
>   of this pilgrimage;
> Struggle against it, not for one fraction of a moment
>   concede its dominion.
> It will occasion you grief and sorrow; it will torment
>   you.
> But hate not God, nor turn from Him in shame or self-
>   reproach;
> He has seen many such; His compassion is as great as
>   His Creation.
> Be tempted and fall and return, return and be tempted
>   and fall
> A thousand times and a thousand, even to a thousand
>   thousand.
> For out of this tribulation there comes a peace,
> deep in the soul and surer than any dream.[1]

- "If I forgive myself, I will lose the leverage needed to keep myself in line."

  I would like to challenge the underlying assumption that force is what changes people. It is not force but love that changes us. God is in the process of loving the evil out of you; your job is to collaborate with Him toward that end.

- "Maybe God could forgive me, but the person I hurt surely could not."

  There are two parts to this matter. First, God reserves to Himself the right to forgive all sins, having paid for all sins in the death of His Son. But second, how do you know that person could not forgive you? You have to go and ask. It is amazing how few times someone refuses to forgive a person who comes asking for forgiveness. The mere display of humility in the asking frees the offended one to respond with graciousness.

And, yes, you *can* do it, even though you shrink from the prospect of doing so. You can do whatever God tells you to do because He enables you to. You just do not feel the enabling until it is all over. That is how this business works.

- "I will pay for it myself."

Yes, you might. As C. S. Lewis observed, "There are only two kinds of people in the end: those who say to God, 'Thy will be done,' and those to whom God says, in the end, '*Thy* will be done.' All that are in Hell choose it."[2] Either Jesus Christ pays off your sin or you do. But for you to do so means going to hell. On this earth, only Jesus qualified to be a payment for sin; you do not. He spent six hours on the cross paying off the sins of all mankind. You could spend six years on a cross and it would not pay off a single sin.

The Principle of Conditionality

Let me pounce on the main point of this section right at the outset: In several of Jesus' comments, there is an unassailable connection between forgiving and being forgiven. Immediately after teaching the Lord's Prayer, He comments: "For if you forgive men when they sin against you, your heavenly Father will also forgive you. But if you do not forgive men their sins, your Father will not forgive your sins" (Matthew 6:14–15). It would appear, then, that our forgiveness by God is conditioned on our forgiving those who have sinned against us.

On the basis of Jesus' statements, I am saying that forgiveness that has been given *can be rescinded.* If we do not allow His forgiveness to touch our hearts so that we extend forgiveness to others, then His forgiveness of us is conditional, rescindable. Now, does that extend to salvation? This is one place where my thesis of three positions in the afterlife comes into play—the damned, the saved and the rewarded. At best, the unforgiven could be said to be saved but not rewarded to the degree that they withheld forgiveness from others. Once it is understood that forgiveness is an act of the will, there is no excuse for withholding it from others.

This is exactly the point of the parable of the unmerciful servant in Matthew 18. In verse 27 we see forgiveness given: "The servant's master took pity on him, canceled the debt and let him go." When this forgiven servant fails to forgive his fellow servant, his forgiveness is rescinded:

> Then the master called the servant in. "You wicked servant," he said, "I canceled all that debt of yours because you begged me to. Shouldn't you have had mercy on your fellow servant just as I had on you?" In anger his master turned him over to the jailers to be tortured, until he should pay back all he owed.
>
> This is how my heavenly Father will treat each of you unless you forgive your brother from your heart.

> verses 32–35

Get hold of the reality of conditionality. Conditionality is indicated by the words *if, unless* and *as*. There are many *ifs* in the Bible. *If* means that you have the privilege of choice to work *with* God or *against* Him. *If* requires that you take action in order to free up God's blessings or turn aside His judgments. *As* is a small word in English but a huge word in spirituality. The Greek word for *as* is ωσ (*hoos*), which means "just as," "to the same degree," "for the same purpose." It occurs in the Lord's Prayer: "Forgive us our debts, *as* we also have forgiven our debtors" (Matthew 6:12).

Conditionality comes into play on the Day of Judgment. I have a rather gross image that helps to illustrate this point. In the first church where I served, there was a commercial toilet that had a problem. Sometimes air got caught in the pipe, and when it was flushed, the contents spewed back out with a roar instead of going into the sewer. Similarly, every time we confess a sin, the lid of forgiveness opens a bit and our sin is tossed into God's holding tank. While in there, our sin is out of God's view and out of our view. "When I forgive, I forget" is the Lord's gracious message, as noted above. But those sins are not yet totally destroyed. They are unremembered so long as the person forgives others. How God could remember them after having forgotten, I do not know. But it is certainly within His capabilities. He chooses to forgive or He chooses to remember based on our response to having been forgiven.

On the Day of the Lord—the Day of Judgment—one of two things will occur: (1) our guilt will be sealed away from us forever or (2) our guilt will be regurgitated on us to the degree that we have withheld forgiveness from others. We determine which will occur.

One way of summing this up would be to say that salvation is not enough. That is why I have underlined Luke 6:46: "Why do you call me, 'Lord, Lord,' and do not do what I say?" Besides saying "Jesus is Lord" we must move on into obedience to His Word.

Paul's version of this is stated in many places, for example in Romans 5:10: "For if, when we were God's enemies, we were reconciled to him through the death of his Son, how much more, [1] having been reconciled, [2] shall we be saved through his life!" We enter salvation [1] but must also continue to appropriate the grace to walk in the light [2]. Not to do [2] is to jeopardize [1]. Romans 8:3 reads: "And so he condemned sin in sinful man [1], in order that the righteous requirements of the law might be fully met in us [2]."

What I am saying is that the justified will show it. Paul clearly indicates that salvation will work itself out in heart change. And if it is not shown, there is a real question whether it was there in the first place or not. This is in line with those teachings of

Jesus that I have highlighted in this book. Theology must stack up with the Word.

The utter fairness of God will prevail. If He decides that someone who could forgive refused, then that person will suffer loss. They may be saved but not totally happy in the afterlife. The paradox here is that utterly free grace demands responses—belief, generosity, forgiveness, etc. It could be said, "Grace is utterly free, costing not less than everything."

An example of a Bible character who had a hard time with forgiveness is the prophet Jonah, whom God had a hard time getting to Nineveh, the modern city of Mosul in northern Iraq. God wanted to forgive the Ninevites. Jonah was not cooperating. But God's discipline finally had a good effect and Jonah went and preached to the Ninevites. They immediately repented so God immediately forgave them. But Jonah was angry with God for His mercy. "Are you right to be so angry?" God asked. "Yes, I am angry enough to die," Jonah replied. Had he in fact died in that state, he would have found himself ladened with the burden of his own sin. I think he would have been in trouble with God, for he was unwilling to forgive the Ninevites.

What if you get to the pearly gates and find that your own unforgiveness has blackballed you from the fullness of what God had in mind for you? You will be astoundingly anguished.

Common Objections to Forgiving Others

What I have shared above ought to be enough motivation to lead you to forgive others freely. But people raise objections to forgiving others. I want to mention a few of them in order to help you free yourself from their negative influence.

- "Who will repay?"

  Part of the Old Testament law, which still operates in the hearts of many, is the idea of retribution—an eye for an eye. Jesus clearly canceled that idea, but some aggrieved sense of justice can move people to seek revenge or at least repayment. And something in the human nature tends to *overpay* the offender. Look at Israel and Palestine these days. Both peoples overpay the other for every transgression, so continued escalation of conflict is guaranteed. What is God's answer? "Do not take revenge, my friends, but leave room for God's wrath, for it is written: 'It is mine to avenge; I will repay,' says the Lord" (Romans 12:19). Only God can repay fairly, so we should leave it to Him.

- "It is not fair!"

On two occasions Jesus quoted Hosea 6:6. The first time He said, "But go and learn what this means: 'I desire mercy, not sacrifice'" (Matthew 9:13). Mercy, not retribution, is what sets things right. Be careful of hollering for justice—you might just get it. It would not taste good. Seek instead to work with God for the softening of your heart so that it sees mercy as a high virtue. Here is the second time Jesus referenced Hosea 6:6: "If you had known what these words mean, 'I desire mercy, not sacrifice,' you would not have condemned the innocent" (Matthew 12:7). In these two occasions of quoting Hosea, Jesus uses the words *learn* and *known*. Mercy is a learned commodity. We grow up into it.

- "He has not repented."

Jesus' example on the cross is worthy of emulating: "Father, forgive them, for they do not know what they are doing" (Luke 23:34). He did not wait until they repented in order to forgive. Forgiveness puts one in the driver's seat instead of waiting for the other person to get around to repenting.

- "He needs to be stopped from hurting others."

In this stance we can try to hold the offender accountable for the sake of the damage he might do to others. Maybe so. But it would be best to approach the matter from Jesus' perspective instead of our own. What did He say to

111

do? "If your brother sins against you, go and show him his fault, just between the two of you" (Matthew 18:15). That is step one. Step two: "But if he will not listen, take one or two others along." Step three: "If he refuses to listen to them, tell it to the church." Step four: "If he refuses even to listen to the church, treat him as you would a pagan or a tax collector."

I have never gotten to step three. Step one or two has taken care of the problem every time.

The problem with the disobedient people of God is that they reverse the order of the steps. To start with step three or four is to take an affront and escalate it to the level of war with the insistence that people take sides. Instead of a one-on-one conflict being redeemed through confrontation and forgiveness, the matter quickly becomes group-against-group. This is not forgiveness, it is not reconciliation, it is not mercy and it is not the will of God.

You know what is even more interesting? Almost every time I have gone alone to those who have offended me, I have heard the matter from their side and have ended up asking forgiveness for *my* having judged *them*. When I saw it from their perspectives, my misreading of their intent became apparent.[3]

- "How often do I have to do this?"

At least 77 times (Matthew 18:22). In other words, keep doing it. Over and over again.

- "I would be lying if I said I forgave him."

I had the privilege of being the spiritual director at a women's retreat a number of years ago. A week or so after it concluded, Martha, a participant, called to ask if I would visit her in order to pray for her multiple sclerosis. After I arrived, I interviewed her about the condition. It soon became apparent that her illness was connected to what sounded like justified anger at her ex-husband.

"Oh," I said finally, "you have to forgive him."

"Then I am going to stay sick!" Martha replied vehemently.

"Well, hold on a sec here," I replied. "Let me show you something." Then I drew on a napkin this little graph:

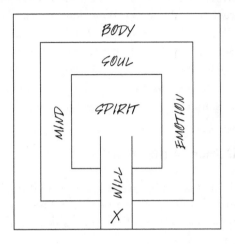

"You think faith has to operate in your emotions and that you have to feel what you are trying to have faith about."

"Don't I?"

"No, God has not placed faith in the emotions. Nor has He placed it in the intellect. You do not have to feel faithful; nor does something God wants you to do have to make sense to your reason. Where God has placed faith is in the will, where that 'X' is. What the will does is make decisions. Just *decide* to forgive him."

After we discussed this for a couple of minutes, she suddenly bowed her head.

"Lord, *if* what Mike says is true, then I *willfully* forgive my ex-husband. And You know that I do not *feel* it, God, and it does not seem to be a very good idea either. Amen."

Well, she had satisfied my requirements, so I prayed for her. Three days later she called to say that her symptoms had entered a 98 percent remission.

Cool, huh? That God has made faith a matter of will protects our emotional and intellectual integrity while still allowing us to have effective faith. We do not have to say that we feel like doing something He wants us to do, nor do we have to pretend that it makes perfect sense to our reason. In my experience, in fact, the feelings and the understanding come *after* the act of faith, not before.[4]

So one does not have to feel forgiving in order to forgive. Just do it, and let the feelings take care of themselves.

The Condition of the Heart

What is at stake in forgiveness is the condition of the heart. Jesus wants us to have clean hearts, unburdened by our own sins or the sins of others. Forgiveness is what allows Him to clean them.

Let me tell you the story of Dora. When I first met her, Dora, in her midfifties, was supporting her family by cleaning houses. We met at Cursillo—a weekend program for spiritual renewal—where I was a leader. We liked each other right off the bat. At the closing ceremony I felt honored to present a cross made of nails to Dora, as the hundred others present chanted in unison, "Fear not, Dora, for I have redeemed you; I have called you by name and you are Mine" (see Isaiah 43:1). Dora hung that cross on a chain to wear around her neck.

Soon after, she began coming to the church I pastored. As busy as she was, she regularly showed up at Bible studies and prayer meetings, as well as Sunday morning worship. I liked her because she was transparently real. There was no pretense about her. She was never arrogant. If she had a problem, she described it in straightforward terms. She knew and loved and served Jesus.

Several years later she went on vacation with my family one summer. Joel, our youngest, was only one or two years old, and Dora had offered to come along and help tend him. We went camping in a small tent trailer with an adjoining tent into which we crammed the seven of us and all our stuff. After we had camped our way up the foggy coast of California, we stopped at Big Sur, where we spent several days. Then after breakfast one day we broke camp, and I announced that we were going to head inland for Clear Lake in order to warm up. As I mentioned the route we would take, I noted that we would pass through Salinas. Suddenly Dora grew very still. As I looked into her wonderful face, I saw that she was in a bit of shock.

"Dora," I said, "what's wrong?" But she just shook her head and turned away. Refusing to be put off, I pursued her.

"What is it?" I demanded gently.

"I had no idea we would be going anywhere near Salinas. I did not even know where Salinas was."

"What is so important about Salinas?"

Her face went through several swift changes before she said, "That is where my dad is buried."

And I knew that this was a divine appointment, for Dora's father had abandoned her and the rest of the family when she was a young girl. The years of misery into which his abandonment had propelled them was beyond description. When he did resurface periodically over the years, pain was added to pain. Later, her husband followed the model of her father and left her to raise their three children. Though she was a gifted vocalist, Dora was never able to pursue her singing career. When her father died, the family learned that he was buried in Salinas.

Arriving in Salinas shortly after noon, we got a motel room, and then Dora and I began tracking down where her father could have been buried. I kept sneaking looks at Dora to see how she was doing. Her face mostly evidenced a large impassiveness, but I knew there was more going on behind that look.

By midafternoon we had learned that he was buried in a pauper's field owned by the county. With the number of his grave site in hand, the two of us went looking for the place. Pretty soon we were wandering through the rows of graves in a weed-covered field, each marked with a serviceable metal stake pounded to ground level and covered with a metal tag imprinted with the number of the deceased. Unless you looked closely, there was nothing to indicate that this was a burial ground. I hung back, letting Dora take the lead and watching her for any distress. Presently we came to the spot.

Dora knelt down and pruned the weeds away from the humble marker. There was no name, no headstone, no flowers, no artwork—nothing at all that honored or even remembered the man whose remains were interred there. Gently she cleaned the site, performing for her father that service she performed for so many.

Finally she looked up at me with tears in her eyes and said, "There isn't anything here to make this special." With those words I knew that she had come through to victory. If ever a woman had a right to vindictive spite, it was she, but instead she responded with grace. That simple, plaintive statement held forgiveness, resolution, faith and maturity.

Dora's maturity, you see, enabled her to be free. Having to confront her father exposed a growing, mature faith that allowed her to act like Jesus toward him. While surprised by stumbling across Salinas, she was not thrown by it. In fact, she ended up saying, "Praise God that He arranged for me to go to Salinas and release my dad into peace"—her peace, at least, and maybe his as well.

So we set about tidying up the grave site, pulling weeds, smoothing over the soil and even bordering it with a few stones we found. We said prayers—tearful, grateful prayers. Then, in a spontaneous act that symbolized all that had happened, Dora took off her Cursillo cross of nails and plunged it into the ground by the marker. It was her final act of forgiveness and freedom. Her heart was clean, unburdened, free—just the way Jesus wanted it.

The Process of Forgiving

Forgiveness is a process that comprises a number of steps. In order to willfully forgive someone who sins against us, it is helpful to take the following steps to forgiveness.

1. *Awareness of the offense.* At some point, we become aware that someone has sinned against us. The awareness of the sin can develop over either a short or long period of time.

2. *Optional: Confront the offender.* Often you can settle the matter between God and yourself by telling Him that you are forgiving the one who hurt you. But if that does not close the matter in your heart in a week or so, you may have to ask the Lord, "Do You want me to confront that person as Matthew 18 teaches?" If you get a sense that the Lord is saying yes, then pluck up your courage and make an appointment to see that person.

When you are face-to-face, you might say something like this: "I read Matthew 18 where Jesus instructs us to talk to someone we think has sinned against us. I want to tell you the effect that one of your behaviors had on me. [Tell him/her.] Now, was it your intention to hurt me? Because if it was, I want to forgive you. If it was not your intention to hurt me, I would like you to consider changing this particular behavior in the future so that I will not read it as an intent to harm."

What about when you are the offender? Jesus said that if we are offering our gift in church and remember that someone has something against us, we should put our gift aside, be reconciled to the one we offended and then come and offer our gift. You might say something like this: "Remember last week when I did/said something to hurt you? My conscience has been bothering me about it, and I want to ask your forgiveness. Would you forgive me?"

These acts are uncomfortable, no question about it. But "uncomfortable" does not mean "impossible." When you set out to do something difficult in obedience to Jesus, He swings into action to bless what you do.

3. *Send the sin away.* The Hebrew and Greek words that are translated "forgive" literally mean to "dismiss" or "send away." The Bible helps us understand this concept by using distance images: *"As far as the east is from the west,* so far has he removed our transgressions from us" (Psalm 103:12). "You will again have compassion on us; you will tread our sins underfoot and hurl all our iniquities *into the depths of the sea"* (Micah 7:19). These images of how God forgives our sins should be our model for how we should forgive others. Just send the person's guilt far away. Dismiss it. In other words, do not allow it to sit between the two of you any longer.

If it is your own sin you are trying to send away, your mind will likely inform you that you are a special case and that it is not working for you. You will have accusatory thoughts and continued feelings of guilt. Just renounce those thoughts and reaffirm your decision that God and you have forgiven you. Then remind yourself that you will feel the forgiveness at some point in the future, but you are not going to disbelieve that you are forgiven just because you do not yet feel it.

4. *Forget it.* God forgets sin and you should, too. Simply refuse to think about it when it pops into your consciousness. Eventually it will give up and stop knocking on the door of your mind.

5. *Understand who the real enemy is.* Jesus and St. Paul clearly inform us that the real enemy is not the person who sinned against you, but the devil (Ephesians 6:12; 1 Peter 5:8). You are never exhorted to forgive the devil, but you are commanded to forgive people whom he motivates to sin against you.

6. *Remind yourself of the dynamics of forgiveness.*

- *Trust.* Trust that God is a God of justice and will see that justice ends up being done or that mercy fully meets justice's requirements.
- *Understand the cross.* Jesus came to earth to pay for mankind's sins. To excuse oneself from forgiving is to insult His purpose and His sacrifice.

- *Obedience.* We should willfully comply with the commands of Jesus to forgive.
- *Largeness of heart.* The heart is always the Lord's target. Every time you obey Him, your heart grows more like His.
- *Self-denial.* We must control the thoughts and feelings that would defy Jesus' command to forgive. This may feel like and actually be self-denial.
- *Love.* "Love is a decision," someone accurately said. When you make the decision to love someone by forgiving him, you grow in love.

Let me sum up the subtleties of the process of true forgiveness through a lengthy quote from George MacDonald.

A man will say: "I forgive, but I cannot forget. Let the fellow never come in my sight again." To what does such a forgiveness reach? To the remission or sending away of the penalties which the wronged believes he can claim from the wrong-doer.

But there is no sending away of the wrong itself from between them.

Again, a man will say: "He has done a very mean action, but he has the worst of it himself in that he is capable of doing so. I despise him too much to desire revenge. I will take no notice of it. I forgive him. I don't care."

Here, again, there is no sending away of the wrong from between them—no *remission* of the sin.

A third will say: "I suppose I must forgive him; for if I do not forgive him, God will not forgive me."

This man is a little nearer the truth, inasmuch as a ground of sympathy, though only that of common sin, is recognized as between the offender and himself.

One more will say: "He has wronged me grievously. It is a dreadful thing to me, and more dreadful to him, that he should have done it. He has hurt me, but he has nearly killed himself. He shall have no more injury from it that I can save him. I cannot feel the same toward him yet; but I will try to make him acknowledge the wrong he has done me, and so put it away from him. Then, perhaps, I shall be able to feel toward him as I used to feel. For this end I will show him all the kindness I can, not forcing it upon him, but seizing every fit opportunity; not, I hope, from a wish to make myself great through bounty to him, but because I love him so much that I want to love him more in reconciling him to his true self. I would destroy this evil deed that has come between us. I send it away. And I would have him destroy it from between us, too, by abjuring it utterly."[5]

That is true Christian love demonstrated in the act of forgiveness.

The Power of Forgiveness

Forgiveness not only dismisses sin but also allows a number of other blessings from God to take place. To conclude this chapter, let's look at those blessings.

• *Healing.* Remember Martha with multiple sclerosis? Her healing came from releasing her ex-husband from her ire. I have an interesting follow-up to that story. About six months after I had visited her, she showed up in my living room as the guest of a woman who was living with us. As we got reacquainted, I asked, "How's the M.S.?"

She looked a bit sheepish and said that it was troublesome again.

So I said, somewhat slyly, "And how has your 'ex' been treating you?"

"He is still doing everything he can to upset me," Martha replied.

"Have you renewed your forgiveness of him to take into account the new offenses?" I asked.

A light came into her eyes. "I'll take care of it, Pastor!" she replied rather assertively. We laughed and I said, "Okay, go for it."

When she got home that night, she knelt beside her bed and said something like this: "O God, George is still being an

S.O.B., so I forgive him for the things he has done since the last forgiveness." She listed his offenses, forgiving each one, and then got into bed. She woke up symptom free the next morning. This experience taught her that healing can be an indicator of forgiveness and, inversely, that illness can be an indicator of unforgiveness.

A colleague, Doug Gregg, and I wrote a book entitled *Inner Healing* about ten years ago. Looking back through it, I count dozens of times we used the word *forgive*. And often when we conduct conferences and pray for the sick, we find ourselves gently bringing up the matter of forgiveness. Generally when people forgive those who hurt them, they receive measurable healing. Forgiveness cancels resentment, which has a way of doing a U-turn and afflicting our own bodies. Forgiveness is especially important to our emotional health and is key to being healed of emotional hurts, fears and guilt.

• *Redemption.* In Ephesians 1:7–8 Paul says, "In him we have redemption through his blood, the forgiveness of sins, in accordance with the riches of God's grace that he lavished on us with all wisdom and understanding." When forgiveness is going on, God's redemptive purposes are being fulfilled.

• *Cleansing.* "If we confess our sins, he is faithful and just and will forgive us our sins and purify us from all unrighteousness" (1 John 1:9). It is wonderful to be cleansed of sin. Sin is a defiling, dirtying factor. When we confess our sins and lay hold of God's forgiveness, He washes us. He is so good at washing that even the memory of sin and its stain begins to ebb away.

• *Justification.* St. Paul also uses this word to describe what Christ has done for us on the cross. You were guilty; now you are not. Jesus paid for your sins through His death and resurrection, and this act, which brought about God's forgiveness, also accomplished your justification. Someone made a pun on the word "justified," saying "it is 'just as if I'd' never sinned."

• *Expansion of God's Kingdom.* In the next chapter we will see some of the dimensions of the Kingdom of God. For the moment, we should recognize that each forgiveness extends the borders of His reign. This is also true of each healing. In the healing of a paralytic, Jesus used both: "'But that you may know that the Son of Man has authority on earth to forgive sins. . . .' He said to the paralytic, 'I tell you, get up, take your mat and go home.' He got up, took his mat and walked out in full view of them all. This amazed everyone and they praised God, saying, 'We have never seen anything like this!'" (Mark 2:10–12). The healing proved the forgiveness, and both made a great impact on those who witnessed them.

• *Release from bondages.* In the first three verses of Ephesians 2, St. Paul uses these phrases: "dead in your transgressions," "followed the ways of this world," "gratifying the cravings of our sinful nature," "objects of wrath." Then: "But because of his great love for us, God, who is rich in mercy, made us alive with Christ even when we were dead in transgressions—it is by grace you have been saved" (verses 4–5). Hundreds of people with whom I have interacted have been released from the things that bound them by coming into God's arms. Guilt, self-condemnation, poor self-image, addiction, hatred, compulsivity, joylessness—in all of these things forgiveness has been a key to release and healing.

• *Heart change.* Zacchaeus was a traitor. He collected taxes from his own people for the oppressive government and filled his own pockets by overcharging. But when Jesus invited Himself to his home for lunch, Zacchaeus was so touched that he declared, "Look, Lord! Here and now I give half of my possessions to the poor, and if I have cheated anybody out of anything, I will pay back four times the amount" (Luke 19:8). This is heart change! And Jesus sealed the change when He summed up, "Today salvation has come to this house, because this man, too, is a son of Abraham. For the Son of Man came to seek and to save what was lost" (verses 9–10). Has your heart been changed by being forgiven? What about by extending forgiveness to someone else?

• *Freedom for the forgiver.* When someone sins against us, we carry the burden of the other's sin. It clings to us until we dismiss it through forgiveness. Until we free its hold on us, we are compelled to turn control of our lives over to those who have hurt us. But through forgiveness, we gain freedom from their act. Then it no longer has power to control, manipulate, direct or influence us. Remember my story in chapter 3 of fasting and praying one day for an enemy? In one day of God-directed prayer for this person, I was completely released from all negative factors in that relationship. Now, whenever I think of that person, I send warm blessings toward him with a sincere heart. I am free.

• *Clears out hindrances to the operation of grace.* When we forgive, we dismiss whatever blocks that the world, the flesh or the devil have implanted in us. This frees the grace of God to move through us with capability and effect. "Mercy triumphs over judgment!" (James 2:13). If the grace of God does not seem to flow through you as effectively as in the past, you may need to ask yourself if you are carrying bitterness toward anyone.

• *Makes us vulnerable again.* You might not think this is so good. But when we forgive, we open ourselves to the possibility of future hurt by the person we forgave. This is good? Yes, for vulnerability to others is crucial to effective relationship. No vulnerability, no relationship.

• *A key to answered prayer.* Jesus gave this advice in Mark 11, "Therefore I tell you, whatever you ask for in prayer, believe that you have received it, and it will be yours. And when you stand praying, if you hold anything against anyone, forgive him, so that your Father in heaven may forgive you your sins" (verses 24–25). Jesus could not talk about prayer very much without talking also about forgiveness. God is able to answer the prayers of those who forgive. God delights to answer the prayers of those who forgive. Forgiveness puts one in full collaboration with the One who is capable of answering prayer.

• *Allows fresh starts to occur.* When I was in my midforties, I wrote these words:

"If I were God, I would have blow-torched me off the face of the earth thirty years ago!" This thought came to me one day while I was repenting of my sins. I was red-faced about my recent sins. I had repented of the very same sins innumerable times before. "Isn't there a limit," I thought, "to how many times He can forgive?" Oh, I knew the passage about 70 times 7, but I was expressing my emotion at the moment instead of my knowledge. I have always been alarmed about the recurrence of my past sins. Every time I read something about "holiness" I come under condemnation because I am not getting very holy. "Where is the 'victory over sin' that is promised? Why am I so weak?" I often lament. "Why does the Lord continue to use me when I am such a lousy sinner?"

I have since gained victory over the sins that I had in mind when I wrote those words. But the learning I was writing about was that our God is the God of fresh starts, and that is as real today as it was then. We human beings are not quick to change. I am impressed at how slow I am to genuinely change. I am equally impressed with how long it takes people who have been abused to be healed to the point where they can change their behaviors. We are slow-moving creatures, a fact concealed by the pace of our lives. We do not get messed up very quickly, and we do not get unmessed very quickly either. It is crucial, therefore, to put our hope, our expectations and our attention onto the living and merciful God. I think that sin does not distress God as much as ignorance of His mercy.

Use every fresh start you need. Never give up using them. Never. And by degrees and unexpected graces you will find eventually that you do not commit those same sins anymore. It happens almost without your notice.

• *Deepens repentance.* David's fifty-first Psalm is a good example of repentance that deepened as it went along. At first he described his sin as "transgression," then as "iniquity" and finally as "bloodguilt." David grew more and more honest—with himself and with God—about his sin. God is eager that His mercy plumb to the depths of our sin, eradicating all of it. As we confess our sin, we may find that we need to say a bit more about it and maybe—in extreme cases—more than that. This is the Spirit enabling us to become totally honest about the thing we have done so that we can be totally forgiven.

• *Destroys the work of Satan.* First John 3:8 summarizes Jesus' ministry: "The reason the Son of God appeared was to destroy the devil's work." Satan is the author of sin. When he gets us to sin, he has promoted the kingdom of darkness. When we forgive, the border of Satan's kingdom is pushed back and the Kingdom of God occupies that territory. Forgiveness is first on the list of weapons in Jesus' hand to destroy the devil's work.

• *Fulfills our commission from God.* God has commissioned each believer to cooperate with Jesus' work of redemption. Each time we forgive ourselves or others, we collaborate in redemption. Forgiveness is one of the chief means that God uses to soften hearts of unbelief. It appeals to the core of one's being. It invites and enables response. It wins by losing, because it circumvents the resistances to it. When you forgive an unbeliever, you free the Spirit of God to wriggle through the chinks in his armor against God.

For many years I have admired this story:

Years ago in the course of their missionary work, Harold Hestekind and his wife were riding bicycles on a busy street in Shanghai, China. She was struck by a bus and thrown beneath it. Mrs. Hestekind was rushed to a hospital, where a head wound was treated. Then investigating officers—with the driver in tow—said to her, "The driver of the bus was entirely to blame for the accident. If you will sign these papers, we will take him into custody."

"No, no," said she. "I don't want to hold him responsible. Let him go free. And please see that he does not lose his position."

The driver looked in amazement at Mrs. Hestekind. Weeping, he said, "My father, mother, brothers and sisters are all Christians, but I have never before seen its attraction. It is love! It is forgiveness! Now I want to give myself to Christ."[6]

125

In summary, then, these are the blessings that result from the glorious power of forgiveness: healing, redemption, cleansing, justification, expansion, release, heart change, freedom, clearance, vulnerability, answered prayer, fresh starts, deepening, destroying Satan's work and fulfillment of our commission.

Forgiveness: Entering God's Heart

When you will to forgive, in obedience to the command to forgive, you set loose in your heart the power of God to enable you to forgive. The oneness with God that the willing to forgive sets loose is itself a greater positive than the negative done by the sin of the other against you. For forgiveness is at the very center of the heart of God. To forgive is to enter His heart.

Why was the unmerciful servant in Matthew 18 condemned? Because he failed to forgive. But why did he fail to forgive? Because he never let his own forgiveness join his heart to the heart of the master. He thought the master was a fool for forgiving him. He took the master's forgiveness as an unexpected boon upon which he capitalized by demanding what was owed to him by his fellow servant. Not only was he set free from an astounding debt, but also—aha!—he could now get a bit ahead by exacting what was owed him out of the other servant. It was all scheming, cerebral, cold-based reasoning. It never touched his heart.

Are victimization issues and justice issues and damage issues and codependency issues important? Yes. They are important enough never to be satisfactorily dealt with on the near side of forgiveness. You will never understand how to deal with them until you forgive. By saying this I do not mean to be simplistic, and I cannot deal here with the issues mentioned. But forgive, and you will find grace to deal with those matters successfully.

Forgive—and Celebrate!

In the Episcopal Church, the presiding clergyperson at a Communion service is called a celebrant. It did not seem very celebratory to me, so one day I asked the Lord, "Just what are we celebrating?" The answer came: *You are having a party of the forgiven.* I have never forgotten that. A Communion service is a party of the forgiven who are celebrating that they have been forgiven. That realization changed the way we did church.

Every denomination's Communion format centers on Jesus' saying over the bread, "This is my body given for you; do this in remembrance of me." And over the cup He said, "This cup is the new covenant in my blood, which is poured out for you" (Luke 22:19–20). As we remember His sacrifice for us, as we recall the wiping out of our sins, as we recollect the vastness of God's mercy toward us, we simply must have a party. We must celebrate. We must rejoice. We must give celebratory expression to the freedoms that have been won for us.

But the party will abruptly end unless we also rejoice in the forgiveness of those who have sinned against us. You have the high privilege of working with the King of kings and the Lord of lords. Just forgive every sin against you. Put it to flight. Banish it from your heart and your memory. Declare it null and void. Stop its negative effects dead in its tracks. Strip it of its strength. Do this by willful forgiveness. Do this and you will live.

Not only will you live, but others will also. Remember, you are the representative of Christ to the world, and few things demonstrate His character as powerfully as forgiveness.

7

The Second Command: *Believe*

"Let Me Help Your Belief"

To believe is Jesus' second strongest command. Why? Because belief is what frees God to do all the things for us and through us that He wants to do. Belief—faith—is the key that unlocks His power, mercy, love and everything else. God loves us whether we believe or not. But belief frees Him to enact His love, and it frees us to receive it.

Faith Is an Act of Will

As I have noted, the Lord asked me some years ago, *What good am I if I am not good in you?* That question drove me to faith, because I had little or no ability in and of myself to produce any goodness representative of Jesus.

His question was not "What good are *you?*" The question was "What good am *I?*" If it was my goodness that the Lord was after, I could have tried to produce at least more good than I had previously. But when He asked, "What good am *I?*" I was driven either to despair or to faith. I have no ability to show how good Jesus is. That job is vastly out of my reach. He is too good, too wonderful, too kind, too everything for me to be able to disclose Him by myself.

So the response was either despair or faith. To despair would have been to misread the question's intent. Such a response would have been to look to self for the necessary resources. And quickly assessing my total inability to do that, I would have been propelled into despair. Or I would have written off the whole question as inspired by the previous night's spinach roiling around in my stomach instead of by the Son of God.

But instead I was driven to faith. Now let me remind you about how I usually respond to such challenges. I decided more than thirty years ago that I had better be honest with God. He knows every thought in my mind, every reaction. So I might as well 'fess up and tell Him how it is with me. As I began to mobilize the forces of faith to deal with His question, I was still emotionally rocked by it. So I said something like this: "*What?* Who do You think You are to require that I disclose You adequately to the world? This is not fair. I am no saint. You have asked the wrong guy." I think I went on in this fashion for quite some time. God was silent. He just let me stew as I tried to grapple with this impossible demand.

When God tells me to do something and I react this way, He stays silent. His silence is not disapproval. It is not disengagement. He is just giving me time to process the thing He has said. My joke about it is: "Sometimes He acts like God. It is as though He is saying, 'I have told you what to do. You decide whether or not you are going to do it, but I am not arguing with you about it.'" He must say this with a twinkle in His eye. Then He is remarkably patient as I bounce around reacting to what He has said. He waits for compliance. When I get myself around to doing what He said, He is freed to swing into action to make the thing work.

The price for grappling with His commands is discomfort. No one likes being uncomfortable. But I have found that it is a small price to pay for effectiveness. So I go through my "what ifs" and "oh nos" and "You can't mean its" because Someone said to count the cost of obedience. The greatest cost for me is usually imagining all the ways the thing He is asking me to do can go wrong.

My advice is that you let yourself ask those questions, feel those feelings and think those thoughts. Then take action anyway. Do what He has said. You will not have full emotional agreement or full intellectual assent to the thing you have been asked to do. In fact, your emotions and intellect may actively oppose obedience to the command. So how do we obey with integrity?

Remember the little graph about body, soul and spirit I drew in the last chapter? Its point was that faith is an act of the will. I decided to put it in the previous chapter to give you time to mull it over before getting to this chapter. Mull all you want. And when you have mulled and pondered and questioned as much as you want, you will come to a point of action or inaction. I understand the process. I know what you are going through. But I also know how crucial it is for your future happiness and success that you bring yourself to the point of willful collaboration with the King.

Let me restate something I said earlier, for it is crucial: In order to safeguard your intellectual and emotional integrity, the Lord requires only that an act of faith be *willful*. Of the three major components of the soul—mind, will and emotion—will is the only one over which you have direct governable control. You cannot tell a feeling to feel differently. Nor can you tell your mind to understand something it does not yet understand. But you can exercise your will and do something the Lord is asking you to do. You do not have to feel like doing it. You do not have to comprehend the reasons for it. And God knows all that, of course. That is why I tell Him how I feel and what I think about His orders. I am just being honest. But the bottom line is compliance. And He only looks into my will to see if I am having faith.

What a bummer it would be if I could believe only what I could understand. That would make for a small universe and a small god.

Everyday Faith

The New Testament uses the word *faith* to describe four kinds of faith, meeting four different needs. The first is *the faith,* the doctrines about God and us in which we believe. The second is *saving faith,* that ability to say yes to Jesus Christ's invitation to receive Him. The third is the *gift of faith,* which is a gift of the Spirit and a kind of booster shot that comes periodically to enable you to do something beyond your normal level of faith. The fourth is *everyday faith.* We are going to talk about everyday faith.

Faith is not so much a noun as it is a verb. One does not *have* faith so much as he *does* faith. It is not a possession but a behavior. Or if it is a possession, it is not apparent or actual until it is put into behavior. That is why this book centers on the commands of Jesus. A command requires an action response.

James had a good grasp of this reality: "In the same way, faith by itself, if it is not accompanied by action, is dead. But someone will say, 'You have faith; I have deeds.' Show me your faith without deeds, and I will show you my faith *by what I do*" (James 2:17–18). A couple of verses later, James comments on the patriarch Abraham: "You see that his faith and his actions were working together, and his faith was made complete *by what he did*" (verse 22). His summation in verse 26 is this: "As the body without the spirit is dead, so faith without deeds is dead."

Our question to the Lord, therefore, is always, "What do You want me to do?" When He tells you, go ahead and do the eight-word prayer—O God, O God, O God, O God—but then do what He is telling you. I like the Nike slogan: Just do it!

"Well, *how* do you do it?" someone may ask. The short answer is that "the how" takes care of itself in "the what." What I mean is that when we set foot in motion to do what He tells us, He sets everything in motion to make it work. If we get hung up on the how, we may talk ourselves out of the what and then miss the miracle of His provision.

A few years ago I lived in Denver. One March morning I boarded a plane at Denver International Airport in order to fly to Chicago, where I would transfer to a flight to Ft. Lauderdale in order to do a men's conference. The plane taxied to the end of the runway and sat there. And sat there. Finally the pilot came on the loudspeaker to tell us that the monitor in the cockpit was not working and that they would have to go back and get it replaced. That took ninety minutes. So by the time we got to Chicago's O'Hare airport, my plane for Ft. Lauderdale had long since departed.

I went to the customer service counter. The best they could do was put me on standby for a 9:00 P.M. flight. Well, I was supposed to finish my first speaking session at that time. I finally thought of asking for help. I looked at Jesus in my mind, and He seemed to be pointing to a bank of monitors. As I looked at them, I saw one for Miami flashing with the word "boarding." *Close enough,* I thought, for Miami is only twenty miles from Ft. Lauderdale. Maybe I could get on that plane. So I ran to the other terminal and up to that gate. I puffed to a halt, but nobody was boarding. As I approached the podium, the clerk saw me coming, pursed her lips and shook her head as if to say, *Don't even come here, mister!*

"You are not having a good day," I began as I reached her station.

"You have no idea!" she fumed. Through teeth that could snap nails, she expostulated, "The pilot did not like the jump seat and just walked off with his crew."

Then she glared at me as she said, "And don't even ask. You are not getting on this plane!"

So I looked at Jesus again. He just nodded. So I pursued the matter: "Well, I am what you guys call a 'premier member' of this airline, and it was an equipment failure that got me in this predicament." She softened about 1 percent.

"Look, just put me on the standby list and I will leave you alone."

"Sir," she sighed, "it will not do any good. There are twenty-five people on the standby list in front of you. This is spring break. Everybody wants to go to Florida." But I did not leave, so she sighed again and began to enter my name in the computer.

Suddenly she jerked her head at the computer. Then she went two stations to the left and dragged her supervisor over to her spot.

"I just typed this gentleman's name in the computer and it disappeared from the screen. What does that mean?"

"I don't know," said the supervisor, as she moved to access the keyboard. Moving aside, the first clerk felt something touch her thigh. In slow motion, she extracted a boarding pass . . . looked at it . . . looked at me . . . looked at it and me again twice more and handed it to me with this comment, "You are one lucky customer, mister."

As I received it, I replied, "Well, ma'am, in my business we don't call this luck, we call it grace."

"I don't care what you call it . . ." she began, then, "oh, are you a Christian?" she asked with distaste.

"Yes, ma'am."

"Then you can just go and pray for another pilot."

"Yes, ma'am," I saluted and went off to my seat. You can bet I began praying in earnest. Within 25 minutes, a new pilot and crew boarded and I flew to Florida in time for my event, which God richly blessed.

Now, at no time during this ordeal did I experience comfort until I got on that aircraft. My job was to do what the Lord was saying; His job was to make it work. I learned that Jesus is even Lord of airline computers.

Another way to say this is expressed in Isaiah 59:1: "The arm of the LORD is not too short." Our job is to prove that His arm is not short; His job is to back us up. Think of the situations in which you need the Lord to reveal and deploy His long arm. Needs, problems, opportunities, illnesses, relationships, provisions, complexities. Is His arm long or not? How will the world know? How will you know if you do not periodically have to put Him to the test? Which also puts you to the test.

You know what we will do in heaven? We will remember God's challenges to us and laugh about how much they scared us. Or we may cry because we dodged the challenges and therefore never experienced the proof of His long arm.

One Sunday morning when I was in my thirties, I was in the kitchen of the parish hall before church. Suddenly, as I looked at a huge trash can, I thought the Lord said, *Put this trash can on the altar during the service.* I was aghast. And I was aghast at what the congregation might think, for it was soiled, marked, definitely unceremonial. So I picked it up and hid it in the pulpit where no one could see it. Then, if I chickened out, no one would know the thing was even there.

When it came time for the sermon, I took a deep breath, walked over to the pulpit, took the trash can and put it on the center of the altar. Since I had no reason in my mind for doing such a thing, I turned to the congregation and asked, "What do you think of that?"

There was silence for what seemed like a long time. Finally, a man said, "Well, haven't you told us that we are to put our sins on the altar as we confess them so that God will take them away in forgiveness?"

"Yes," I replied.

"Well, it seems to me that the altar is the place to unload our trash."

Then someone else chimed in saying, "Wow! That makes it real to me that God really forgives me when I ask Him to."

Another said, "Yeah, for my sins are sometimes really trashy."

In another few minutes, they made more than a dozen comments about the grace of our God in taking away our trash. Then a woman stood up. "I am a visitor here. I came hoping that somehow I could be forgiven for a terrible thing I have done." With tears streaming down her face, she said, "I see now by what you have done that even the worst thing can be forgiven."

The congregation preached the sermon that morning. It was one we never forgot. And we never forgot that God has made every provision for taking away the trash of our sins. We ended up writing our sins on slips of paper, wadding them up, throwing them into the trash can and proclaiming that our God had forgiven us.

In this instance God's command to me required an action response. Uncomfortable as I felt about it, I obeyed. As a result, our entire Body was blessed that day beyond ways I could have imagined. I backed up my faith with actions, and my actions then backed up my faith. "You see that his faith and his actions were working together, and his faith was made complete *by what he did*" (James 2:22).

A friend once said in a teaching, "*Faith* is spelled r-i-s-k." Isn't that the truth! Part of the risk is not knowing for sure that He is saying, "Do this" or "Do that." Remember from chapter 2 that you do not get to be sure. You are simply persuaded, because God speaks in a "whis"—not even a whole whisper. If you are doing your best to listen and to obey, you will have to take risks. Often the risk is relatively light. But sometimes it is very weighty, such as whether or not to marry, take a job, move to another state, change careers, etc. You have done these things, haven't you? You have taken significant risks. What I am urging is that you make it a habit to ask God what He wants and take courageous action on what He may say in reply. That is the life of faith—everyday faith.

Factors in Faith

A number of factors come into play in the business of having faith.

• Revelation

This factor is closely related and builds on the discussion in chapter 2 about hearing the Lord. Revelation is a God-based activity that is meant to guide and bless us. Look at this simple graph:

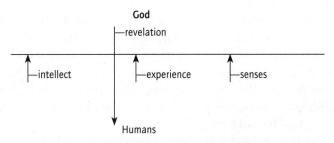

There is a line between God and man. The best that man can do with his reason, experience, senses, education, imagination and guessing is to approach the line. But he cannot pierce through it. None of man's capabilities can discern anything about God's present will for a given situation. Only God can pierce the line, which He does through revelation. But He is eager to give revelation. Recalling our discussion in chapter 2, He gives direction through Scripture, nature, the supernatural, circumstances, others, peace and surprise thinking. All of this He does by the Spirit. That is why I strongly recommended that you ask Jesus for the fullness of the Spirit.

• The Spirit

"The man without the Spirit does not accept the things that come from the Spirit of God, for they are foolishness to him, and he cannot understand them, because they are spiritually discerned" (1 Corinthians 2:14). God can give all the revelations He wants, but unless people are Spirit-enabled, they cannot grasp those revelations. They will be foolishness to them.

We need the humility to come to the Lord for guidance, and we need the humility to ask for the Spirit's assistance in order to apply that guidance. In the Vietnam War a soldier on patrol heard the order "Jump!" which he did, escaping injury from an explosion. When he asked his wounded buddy why he did not jump, his buddy said he had heard nothing. The first was Spirit led; the second was not.

In my first book I spent several pages telling of a fight I had with Jesus over the verse, "Apart from me you can do nothing" (John 15:5),[1] and how He won that fight. Through His victory over me, great and lasting blessings have come to me. One of them has been the humility to know that I need His help. Now I willingly shoot arrow prayers toward Him many times a day asking for His assistance.

The Holy Spirit knows everything about you. He knows exactly how to guide you and how to help you perceive His guidance and take effective action on it. Once you have connected with Him, ask the Spirit for guidance. He yearns to help you.

• *Vital Church Life*

The Reverend Chuck Irish, a mentor of mine, used to say, "Everyone needs three conversions: to Christ, to the Church and to ministry." No one can maintain a vital relationship with Jesus apart from a vital relationship with His Church. This is because Jesus hides Himself in the persons of fellow believers.

Now here we have a problem, for the Church is both the glory and the misery of Christianity. When the Church acts as it should, it shows the glory of Christianity. When it does not, it discloses the misery of Christianity. In other words, the Church is full of people like you—beat up, sinful, selfish and rebellious but also healed, forgiven, changed and redeemed. Because He thinks it is the best way, God has chosen to reveal Himself through this thing called the Church. And I agree with Him. I am sold out to making the local church all that God wants it to be.

All human organizations, including churches, go through a historic pattern, and it is important to be able to discern at which stage a particular church is. The pattern, briefly, is this: First-generation churches are pioneers, full of belief and vigor; second-generation churches coast on and solidify the accomplishments of the first; third-generation churches compromise and settle for mediocrity. Directionally, the pattern travels uphill, levels off and then heads downhill. It can take decades, even generations, for a church to go through all these stages. When you walk into a church you need to ask yourself: Are these folk climbing up, have they leveled off or are they in decline?

Another way to say this is that in first-generation churches Jesus is the actual Head of the Church. He is hands-on. In second-generation or coasting churches, Jesus is the receding Head of the Church. He is hands-on and hands-off. In third-generation or mediocre churches, Jesus is the Head in title only. He is hands-off there.

After a church gets to the third-generation stage, it is confronted with a decision: Renew the vigor of the first generation and head uphill again or defend and rename mediocrity as maturity. But mediocre churches often do not realize they are in mediocrity. They defend mediocrity with intellectual sophistication, eloquent explanation and fervent common sense. But it is all a cover for increasing deadness.

If you find a church in this stage, the best thing would be for you to look for life somewhere else, unless you are already a member of a declining church and the Lord has told you to stay in order to help renew it. You might tell Jesus, "Jesus, lead me to a place and a people where I can find You." Then, go looking.

A living church will look alive. There will be evidence of deep commitment among the people. They will love to worship God. You will see Jesus in the faces of some. You will feel loved there. Even though they do not approve of your sins—which a mediocre church may do—they will let you know they approve of *you*. You will be welcomed and honored. You will be encouraged in your search for Jesus. The place will have the ring of truth about it. It will have vigorous programs that benefit the poor and others beyond their own membership—another sure sign of vitality. Many living churches often utilize a wonderful program called the Alpha Course. In it, they will accept you where you are and help you get to a better place. If you are looking for a church to help you find out about Jesus, ask if they do the Alpha Course. If they have never heard of it, you might take that as an indication of its generational standing.

When I lived in Denver I attended an alive church, Christ Episcopal Church. One year a police detective in our church, Quinn, was investigating the theft of a vehicle. He had to go to Mt. Carmel Baptist Church to interview the owner of the vehicle. As he got to know this man, it came out that their church was in financial trouble. They were full of good works—they provided more than two dozen programs that benefited the poor in their neighborhood—but they had a balloon payment of over thirty thousand dollars that was due on their mortgage in a few weeks, and they had no resources to meet that payment.

Meanwhile, another man in our church, Kit, had a dream in which he saw us giving money to another group. He shared this dream with Sandy, our pastor. With Sandy's encouragement, Quinn and Kit attended worship services at Mt. Carmel the following Sunday. The Sunday after that, these two men stood up in front of our congregation and informed our people of the need of these Baptists. They then claimed that they felt the Lord wanted us to help them with their mortgage and told how our people could participate in it. Over the next several weeks checks earmarked for the Baptists came into the church office. A few Sundays later about twenty of our people went with Quinn and Kit to hand a check to Mt. Carmel for nearly $31,000.

Jubilation broke out in their service as the check was delivered to the pastor. Everybody there vigorously praised God—the givers as well as the recipients. All knew that this was an act of God.

140

Everyone was thrilled to have been a part of something that was truly inspired and achieved by the mercy of God.

A few weeks later the whole congregation of Mt. Carmel came to worship with us at Christ Church as a thank-you. The tears that flowed! The hugs that were shared! This was God and everybody knew it.

These two churches have continued their friendship. A tradition in the Episcopal Church is to wash feet during Holy Week when we remember Jesus' last days on earth prior to His crucifixion and resurrection. You should have seen our pastor, Sandy, washing the feet of the pastor of Mt. Carmel. It was God again.

And what have the Episcopalians received from the Baptists? We found renewed fervor in worship—you ought to hear these Baptists sing!—and friendship between dozens of members. We have a greater willingness to be proactive in racial reconciliation and a renewed passion in ministry to the poor. Jesus has shown Himself truly good to these two churches through each other. That is what He is like. They are two places that are alive, climbing uphill.

How should we relate with these three types of churches?

Like small children, first-generation churches are somewhat messy. They have not been around long enough to have time-tested traditions and resources. They are finding their way. But their vitality will be evident. If God leads you to this kind of church, roll up your sleeves and jump in. They need you. Adopt a posture of flexibility because things may change rapidly. Expect hands-on support from the Head of the Church. You may see healings, miracles and other evidences of God's favor and blessing. Take delight in the fact that you are contributing to the building of something wonderful.

Second-generation churches have more resources. They probably have sufficient buildings in which to house church life. The staff will be a bit more professional in bearing. Larger second-generation churches will have a wide variety of need-meeting programs, and even small churches will attempt to minister to needs. The worship and fellowship may be a bit cooler than in first-generation churches, but it will nonetheless connect you with the living God. It might take longer to find your place in this kind of church.

In third-generation churches, take comfort in knowing that you are not alone. Take comfort in knowing that God loves this church and wants to bless it richly. Take comfort in knowing that the Lord has successfully renewed thousands of churches. Renewal is not easy. I have been involved in the renewal of two congregations. It took everything I had, plus God. But God is deeply interested in renewing His Church.

For many years I was part of a weekly pastors' prayer meeting. At one of our meetings, the Lord showed us a picture of a pie with unevenly sized slices. Each slice represented a demographic group in our city—young marrieds, older retirees, Hispanic singles, etc. Then He showed us that our churches were similarly shaped slices and that each church possessed a God-given ability to appeal to a certain demographic group better than other churches could. Suddenly we realized that it would take the whole Church in our city to minister to the whole city. This helped us realize that we were not in competition with one another. It also helped us realize that we needed every church and every generation to appeal to all the people in our city. No one church could do it all. This realization freed us to bless each other's churches abundantly.

In whatever generation your church is, do the things that Jesus says are important. Six verses from Colossians 3 provide day-to-day guidance:

> Therefore, as God's chosen people, holy and dearly loved, clothe yourselves with compassion, kindness, humility, gentleness and patience. Bear with each other and forgive whatever grievances you may have against one another. Forgive as the Lord forgave you. And over all these virtues put on love, which binds them all together in perfect unity.

Let the peace of Christ rule in your hearts, since as members of one body you were called to peace. And be thankful. Let the word of Christ dwell in you richly as you teach and admonish one another with all wisdom, and as you sing psalms, hymns and spiritual songs with gratitude in your hearts to God. And whatever you do, whether in word or deed, do it all in the name of the Lord Jesus, giving thanks to God the Father through him.

Colossians 3:12–17

Churches are vital to building a faith relationship with Jesus. As I said before, Jesus hides Himself in the persons of fellow believers. Growing your faith, your belief, in Christ is tied inexorably to your growth and your relationships within His Body.

• Experiments of Faith

Another faith-building factor is experiments of faith. From time to time the Lord has challenged me, usually through something He underlines in Scripture. In honesty, I have to say to Him, "I do not know if this will work or not, but I am willing to try an experiment." So I usually set a period of time—a week or two—and do the thing underlined in Scripture without evaluation. When the time is over, I evaluate to see what the results have been. God likes experiments of faith because they free Him to validate His Word and pour out blessings on us.

Has some passage in the Bible been gnawing at you? Does it keep coming to mind? Then turn it into a behavior in which you can engage as an experiment.

Encourage your family and friends to practice faith by exercising their will in agreement with God's Word. Invite them to do it as an experiment and see what happens.

• Taking Control of Our Thoughts

Another factor in faith building has to do with our thoughts. There is a danger among seriously committed Christians to slip into passivity. They think that if they are sold out to Jesus, all they have to do is wait for Him to tell them what to do, what to think and what to say. Watchman Nee describes this person: "He has a mouth but refuses to talk because he hopes the Holy Spirit will speak through it. He has hands but will not engage them since he expects God to do it. He does not exercise any part of his person but waits for God to move him. He considers himself fully surrendered to God; so he no longer will *use* any element of his being."[2] This passivity leads to the loss of self-control and the loss of free will.

Nee continues, "God wants His own to exercise their wills actively to cooperate with Him. This is what is implied in such Scripture verses as: 'if any man's *will* is to do his will, he shall know . . .' (John 7:17) and 'ask whatever you *will*, and it shall be done for you' (John 15:7)."[3] God never violates our will or desires that we place it in His hands. Rather, He wants us to actively use it as the center of our being to collaborate vigorously with Him.

Let's look at the anthropology graph again. The shaded portions—Spirit and Will—indicate those parts of us to which our enemy does not have direct access. But they are his targets, and the arrows indicate ways in which he attacks our spirit and our will.

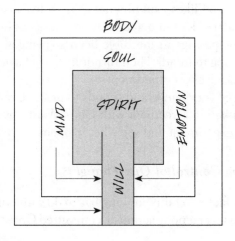

What is a temptation? A thought the enemy uses to get us to make the decision to sin. What are illicit feelings? Simply an addendum to those thoughts designed to emphasize the weight of the temptation. Satan even uses our bodies against us when he can. Has your body ever yearned for something to eat that it should not?

Let me share how to apply this and take control in two areas. The first is taking control of our thoughts in terms of our physical well-being. Over the past nine years I have been engaged in a faith experiment in which I willfully rebuke my own symptoms of illness. I also rebuke any thoughts of acceptance that I am going to get sick, as well as any emotions that accommodate the sickness. Sometimes this is a grit-your-teeth exercise. *I must alert you that on intellectual and emotional levels, it seems futile.* There is little in my thinking or feeling to support that this rebuking stuff is going to do any good. Besides, "rebuking" sounds too zealous for me.

But what I have discovered is that our loving God has equipped us with enough chutzpah to overcome the objections of mind, emotions and symptoms. If we willfully persist in using our authority to rebuke these things for a couple of minutes, over 98 percent of new symptoms disappear within hours. When an illness is thoroughly entrenched, it usually takes longer.

I have staged this for others in conferences. About 80 percent of people's pain flees after just a couple of minutes in which their neighbors lay hands on them and willfully rebuke their pain. When rebuking does not take care of it, we shift to a five-step healing model[4] to sort out the cause of the illness in order to bring God's power against it.

The second area I want to address is taking control of our thoughts, period. I used to be tortured by my thoughts, for I assumed that they were an undeniable and unopposable part of me. I would have a wretched thought of some kind and immediately sink into a rather fatalistic self-condemnation: *How awful I must be to have had such a thought!* I even misapplied the axiom "As a man thinketh, so is he" to justify a hopeless condemnation of myself.

I certainly agree that thinking is crucial. But what I found is that I can take control of my thinking. "Think on these things," Paul exhorts (Philippians 4:8, KJV), and I have found that I can willfully direct my thinking toward the good and away from the evil. When an unworthy thought comes to my mind, now I just say, "Lord, I rebuke that thought and refuse to let it have any influence on me." That takes care of it. The evil thought fizzles away. End of episode. And if a feeling of guilt accompanies the thought, I rebuke that, too.

My task is to bring my thinking into conformity to that of Jesus Christ. How do I know that a thought is unworthy? I read the Book. And I willfully agree with the Book. That frees the Lord to give me peace, joy, power, fun and usefulness.

What kinds of thoughts bother you? We can struggle with thoughts related to temptation; thoughts designed to produce fear in you; thoughts of superiority over others; thoughts of self-condemnation; thoughts that counter the revealed Word of God; thoughts of lust; and thoughts that promote dishonesty. Take authority over them. Do not be passive or fatalistic about them. When you exercise your will against these things, God swings into action to augment your decision, and His power is released against that which is attacking you.

On a more positive note, the full text of Philippians 4:8 reads: "Finally, brothers, whatever is true, whatever is noble, whatever is right, whatever is pure, whatever is lovely, whatever is admirable—if anything is excellent or praiseworthy—think about such things." This is more than "positive thinking," though positive thinking is highly commendable. Rather, this is practicing the mind of Christ. These are the things Jesus thinks about. When we put our minds on the noble, right, pure, lovely, admirable, excellent and praiseworthy, we free Jesus to think His thoughts in our minds, maintain His priorities in our attitudes and bless us by the power enabled by those thoughts.

Good Faith for Bad Times

Into all of our lives come times that test our faith. Troubled times can be divided into many categories: personal, marital, familial, economic, occupational, cultural, regional, national and international. There are trials of health, trials of relationship, trials of belief, trials of natural catastrophes, trials of opposition, trials of war.

It is no good being in denial about trials. They will come. And we do not have to be in denial about them, for we have a God who thoroughly understands them and understands how to help us face them.

No one invites troubled times to come. But they come. The Bible is very realistic about this. It is also very realistic about what to do in difficult times.

Toward the end of his first letter to the Corinthians, Paul exhorted: "Now, brothers, I want to remind you of the gospel I preached to you, which you received and on which you have taken your stand. By this gospel you are saved, if you hold firmly to the word I preached to you. Otherwise, you have believed in vain" (1 Corinthians 15:1–2). The words "hold firmly" indicate that times will arise that shake our faith. Peter spells it out more explicitly: "In this you greatly rejoice, though now for a little while you may have had to suffer grief in all kinds of trials. These have come so that your faith—of greater worth than gold, which perishes even though refined by fire—may be proved genuine and may result in praise, glory and honor when Jesus Christ is revealed" (1 Peter 1:6–7).

James chimes in, "Consider it pure joy, my brothers, whenever you face trials of many kinds, because you know that the testing of your faith develops perseverance. Perseverance must finish its work so that you may be mature and complete, not lacking anything" (James 1:2–4). Jesus also taught plainly about testing times and exhorted us to keep watch, as we addressed in chapter 5. He also warned, "In fact, a time is coming when anyone who kills you will think he is offering a service to God" (John 16:2).

Peter and James were so confident of God's ability to sustain us in difficult times that they exhorted us to "greatly rejoice" and "consider it pure joy." What an attitude! These are the words of people who have learned to look past the immediate trials to the One who is able to bring them through them into "praise, glory and honor" so they will be "mature and complete."

What are the secrets to surviving and even thriving in tough times?

• *Cultivate a general trust in God*—reminding yourself who God is and what His capabilities are. The Psalms are a good guide here. Often when the psalmist is faced with trials, he reminds himself of what God has accomplished in the past. This sets him up for a confident asking for the current need. The New Testament writers could rejoice in the face of adversity because they looked past the adversity into the face of God, who was more than the match for the problem.

• *Refuse to be stampeded.* This is the willful resisting of impulses and evidences that urge one to flee. You do not have to pretend that you see the answer when you do not, but you can remind yourself that God does have the answer and knows how and when to actualize it.

• *Stand firm.* St. Paul declares in Ephesians 6 that our enemy is bigger than we are. The enemy is Satan. But God is bigger than he. So, Paul says, suit up in the armor of God—which I do daily—and then stand your ground. Refuse to be pushed back. When you are under attack, standing your ground is success. Just stand in the strength of God until the crisis blows over.

• *Problem solve.* Once you have done the above, utilize these simple steps to problem solving: (1) identify the problem; (2) determine the cause; (3) decide which solution best fits the cause; (4) put the solution into effect; (5) modify the solution as needed; (6) celebrate the victory when the problem has been successfully solved.

• *Determine to endure.* One of our tenets has to be that God will not allow us to be assaulted beyond our ability—with His help—to endure and triumph over the assault.

• *Grieve.* Attack and counterattack are the two most prevalent activities on the surface of this planet. We are always at war, whether or not countries are in military combat. God and His people attack the reign of Satan through the words and works of Jesus; then Satan counterattacks however he can. In any war there are casualties. When a casualty is close to you, you must grieve. Grieve by honestly acknowledging your loss and celebrate that God holds the trump card of triumph. If there is a death, grieve for your loss but celebrate that God has raised the dead to new and eternal life.

• *Stay anointed in the Spirit.* In biblical times shepherds knew that each spring insects called nose flies afflicted the sheep by laying eggs in the sheep's nostrils. When these hatched, the larva burrowed into the membranes of the nostrils, causing severe burning sensations that caused sheep to bash their snouts against rocks. So the shepherd mixed a batch of oil and sulfur and anointed the nostrils every few days. The nose flies would not land because they did not like the feel of the oil or the smell of the sulfur.

When tragedy comes, the nose flies of despair, questioning, fear and pain attack. At such times, we need Shepherd Jesus to anoint us with the Spirit to get us past these threats to our stability.

• *Stick together.* The book of Ecclesiastes offers sound advice about the strength we get from one another: "Two are better than one, because they have a good return for their work: If one falls down, his friend can help him up. But pity the man who falls and has no one to help him up! . . . Though one may be overpowered, two can defend themselves. A cord of three strands is not quickly broken" (Ecclesiastes 4:9–10, 12). The New Testament echoes this thought in Galatians 6:2: "Carry each other's burdens, and in this way you will fulfill the law of Christ." A wonderful synergy emerges from bearing each other's burdens. Much of the weight on our shoulders is lifted when we exchange burdens with a prayer partner.

• *Practice intimacy with Jesus.* In 1875 a group called the Keswick Convention started a renewal movement in England. A good introduction to the truths of this movement can be gleaned from V. Raymond Edman's book *They Found the Secret.*[5] A forerunner of their teachings was a Scot preacher, Robert M. McCheyne, who crystallized deep truth into two loaded phrases: "Christ *for* us is all our righteousness before a holy God; Christ *in* us is all our strength in an ungodly world." I memorized that sentence long ago and have drawn grace from it many times.

Jesus is what we need in any circumstance. Are you feeling guilty? Jesus supplies your righteousness before the throne of heaven. Are you feeling weak? Jesus supplies your strength to face anything in this world.

Jesus Himself is all the resource you need to live the Christian life. He is of greater worth than gold, and so, says Peter, is your faith in Him. Sometimes we are tempted to think that enough gold would solve all our problems. Not so! You need something far richer than gold. You need Jesus Himself. And He is available.

Make Him your best friend, your close confidant, your immediate resource. Tell Him all the time what a great job He did with creation. Tell Him how honorably He conducted Himself in achieving your salvation. Tell Him what a good job He is doing growing you up. Enjoy Him. Enjoy His enjoyment of you. Rejoice that He has elevated you to the highest levels by recruiting you into active collaboration with Him.

A Word for the Unbeliever

Chances are if you are reading this book, you are already a believer in Jesus. But maybe somebody has handed you this book just for this paragraph.

You have heard that Jesus is the key figure in human history. Even time is broken into segments of before-Him (B.C.) and after-Him (A.D.). But you also have heard of Buddha and Confucius and Mohammed, and you may wonder if it really makes any difference whom you follow. You have heard of faith but you may not know how to go about having faith or in whom to put your faith. You are probably aware that some things need to change in your life. Maybe you are under the control of something that is running you and you need Someone to bust you out of that slavery. Maybe your conscience is bothering you because of the things you have done in the past. Maybe there just is not any real meaning in life as far as you can see at this point. Maybe you do not have the ability to make your relationships work out well. Maybe you keep making the same mistakes over and over and you are digging a deep rut. Maybe you just need a little peace in your heart because you suffer from so much tension or guilt or confusion or inability. Maybe you have achieved all you hoped for and life is still hollow. Whoever and wherever you are, look for Jesus. If He is who He says He is, He will be able to connect with you. Look for Him through the Bible and through His Church—especially the first-generation variety.

8

The First Command: *Love*

"How Good I Am When I Am Loving in You"

I have been yearning to start this chapter since beginning to write the book. This is the peak of the mountain. This is the top command in the teachings of Jesus. There are wonderful blessings for us and for others as we obey this command.

In the great majority of Jesus' use of the word *command* in the gospels, the explicit command is to love. In just three chapters—John 13–15—He uses the word *command* eight times, telling us to love fifteen times (John 13:34; 14:15, 21; 15:9–10, 12–14, 17). The Greek word used most often for *command* is *entole,* which means "to enjoin upon, to give something in charge." Its noun form means "an injunction, charge, precept or commandment."

Jesus is not forcing us to love one another. He always respects our free will, placing Himself in the role of a supplicant. But He is very strongly beseeching us to love.

Let me refresh your appreciation for love by dropping some quotes here:

They [the Christians] know one another by secret marks and signs, and they love one another almost before they know one another. —Statius Caecilius

You can give without loving, but you cannot love without giving. —Amy Carmichael

There is no surprise more wonderful than the surprise of being loved; it is God's finger on man's shoulder. —Charles Morgan

Our Lord does not care so much for the importance of our works as for the love with which they are done. —Teresa of Avila

It is not how much we give but how much we love. —Mother Teresa

Love makes everything lovely; hate concentrates itself on the one thing hated. —George MacDonald

Love is that outreaching power of the imagination which makes real the condition of others. —Fred Roach

Love and laughter form the plough that prepares the ground (the human heart) for the seed. Remember this. If the ground is hard, seed will not grow there. Prepare the ground as I say. —A. J. Russell

Faith is the root and love is the fruit. —Andrew Murray

Love cures people, both the ones who give it and the ones who receive it. —Dr. Karl Menninger

Why Love Is the Top Command

In the world, love is seen as a nice extra but not an essential. "Love!" does not appear at the top of business plans, international law, education formats, military principles or marketing procedures. In the world, you take care of other things first and then put your attention on love. God, however, sees things differently. Not only does He have love, but He *is* love (1 John 4:16). Being and doing love, He wants nothing but the best for us, His beloved creatures. So His top command—even before the arrival of Jesus on earth—is to love.

Seven factors are worth noting when studying this primary commandment of Jesus. We will call them the Seven Ps—the priority, practice, presence, promise, practicality, persuasion and power of love.

The Priority of Love

Someone asked Jesus, "Which is the greatest commandment in the law?" Jesus replied, "'Love the Lord your God with all your heart and with all your soul and with all your mind.' This is the first and greatest commandment. And the second is like it: 'Love your neighbor as yourself.' All the Law and the Prophets hang on these two commandments" (Matthew 22:37–40). This is an extremely economical statement. There are 73 chapters of law in the Old Testament and 245 chapters of prophecy. What is more, at the time of Christ there were 614 laws binding every Jewish citizen. The genius of Jesus is that He crystallized all these writings into two commandments while losing none of their validity.

By doing this, Jesus removed obedience from the cold impersonality of legalism and placed it in the warm personhood of heart. That made obedience a personal relationship rather than an external conformity to rules and regulations. In John 14:21, He claimed, "Whoever has my commands and obeys them, he is the one who loves me." Obedience is relationship with Jesus. And obedience is relationship with each other: "My command is this: Love each other as I have loved you" (John 15:12).

This top priority benefits all. God is blessed by our love toward Him and others. We are blessed by our love toward God and man. Others are blessed by our love toward God and them. That is why it is the priority.

The Practice of Love

In the middle paragraph of 1 Corinthians 13, St. Paul gives us a great functional description of how to love. Here are two translations:

New International Version	New King James Version
4 Love is patient, love is kind. It does not envy, it does not boast, it is not proud.	Love suffers long and is kind; love does not envy; love does not parade itself, is not puffed up;
5 It is not rude, it is not self-seeking, it is not easily angered, it keeps no record of wrongs.	does not behave rudely, does not seek its own, is not provoked, thinks no evil;
6 Love does not delight in evil but rejoices with the truth.	does not rejoice in iniquity, but rejoices in the truth;
7 It always protects, always trusts, always hopes, always perseveres.	bears all things, believes all things, hopes all things, endures all things.

One day it occurred to me to put my own name in the place of the word "love" as a way to make real its application in my life. So I read, "Mike is patient, Mike is kind. Mike does not envy, he does not boast, he is not proud," and so on. This simple technique brings the practice of love alive quickly. Where I felt I had copped out on love, I asked for forgiveness and determined anew to practice true love.

The practice of love is beneficial at every step: planning to love, actually loving and evaluating love's results.

The Presence of Love

The last words of Jesus in Matthew's gospel are the Great Commission. He concluded it by saying, "[Teach] them to obey everything I have commanded you. And surely I am with you always, to the very end of the age" (Matthew 28:20). We have seen that His strongest teaching is to love. As we fulfill that command, His presence materializes to enable and reward us: "I will be with you always." His closest disciple, John, concurs: "God is love. Whoever lives in love lives in God, and God in him" (1 John 4:16). When we love, the presence of God is with us.

One of the things I do is practice the presence of God. Over 25 years ago I decided I would do this on a regular basis—very regular. After trying several different time lengths, I finally landed on 24 minutes. I had in my mind the 24 elders who encircle the throne of God in heaven. They are in His presence, as I seek to be. My watch has a countdown timer, and every day I set the alarm to sound at 24-minute intervals throughout the day. So I play a game with the watch, trying to remember to connect up with the Lord before the alarm goes off. Then when it sounds, I also check in with Him. The awareness of His presence helps me behave in loving ways toward others.

The Promise of Love

St. Paul gives us a glorious promise in three words in 1 Corinthians 13:8: "Love never fails." The Greek words are instructive. The word for *love* here is *agape*—God's sacrificial, unconditional love. The word for *never* is *oudepote,* a quadruple negative having the force of "not (not ever) ever, at no time, nohow." And *fails* is *piptei,* which means to decrease from one level to a lower one. What these three words are saying is that if we love with God's love, it will not fail to achieve 100 percent of its purposes.

This is a glorious challenge. Will you spend the rest of your life proving to your world that love never fails? If you take up that challenge, you will be richly blessed, and so will your world.

The Practicality of Love

Love gets things done. Love changes things. Love is effective. All of the needed changes in my life have come through the love of others.

You will recall from chapter 4 the gift of a rosary to me by a child. That act of love changed me. I experienced a similar change at a men's retreat. After a quiet meditation on Jesus' washing of the disciples' feet in John 13, the leaders of the event went to kneel in front of the participants. They carried a basin, a towel and a pitcher. In silence one of them, Sam, took off my shoes and socks, put my feet in the basin, poured warm water over my feet and gently washed them for a couple of minutes. Then holding one foot up, he took the towel and wiped it dry. Then he dried the other. Finally, he bent over and kissed one of my feet before moving on to do the next man's feet.

I was undone. That silent act of humble, loving attention to the lowest part of me went straight for the jugular of my heart. My pride was blindsided and retreated quickly. My self-rejection could not find anything to say. My judgment of the "servant mentality" was dead and buried. My distaste of being an object of personal attention was supplanted with humility. A few moments of that kind of love made changes that have lasted decades.

Love is extremely practical. First John 3:18 encourages us, "Dear children, let us not love with words or tongue but with actions and in truth." Ask Jesus to show you practical, behavioral ways in which you can love someone else.

The Persuasion of Love

Love is not just the end; it is the means of motivation. No other inducement can compare with love's capacity to motivate. Love does not wait until change occurs before it springs on the beloved; love just washes over the beloved before the beloved deserves it. This is very persuasive! It breaks down resistances to change in the beloved. If you are going to love me whether or not I change, then I am free to change.

At that same men's retreat where Sam washed my feet, they let the participants offer a comment at the end. They had been using a Spanish word to describe these acts of love they were pouring out on us. The word was *palanca,* the root of which means "a lever." The best lever I could think of was a crowbar! These men had pried loose a lot of my hang-ups with the river of love they had poured out on me. So I piped up, "All I want to say is thank God for crowbars!"

A couple of weeks later a crowbar was delivered anonymously to my house. It had been painted gold and mounted on lovely Irish green velvet, framed in a fine wood frame. In the corner was a plaque of wood with these words burned into it: "Thank God for crowbars." As I sat with it in my lap, wave after wave of the love of God washed over me. When the intensity began to diminish, my first thought was: *To whom can I do this?*

That is what love does. It persuades you to pour it out on someone else.

The Power of Love

Most power can be defined as ability or force. And while love is indeed able and forceful, it gets its work done through what looks quite unpowerful. Love's power comes from its vulnerability. If you love me whether or not I change, you are being vulnerable to me. You are "open" to me, which means that you could be hurt by me. That vulnerability has a way of bypassing shields and barriers and oppositions and wriggling into the center of the heart.

"Love the hell out of people!" I used to exhort my congregation. I went on, "It is the only way the hell goes."

A woman was brought to my office by her pastor. She had been so badly abused as a child that she had built thick walls all around her. Nothing and no one could pierce those walls. And I could not either. She was so locked up inside that she had not

159

shed a tear in more than a decade for any reason. But I looked to the Lord and He said, *Sing to her in the Spirit.*

Oh, great! I thought. *What good will that do?* And I fumed inwardly for a moment. What would her pastor think if I did that? What would *she* think? But I had nothing else to go on, so rather nonchalantly I said, "Well, I think I am supposed to sing you a lullaby in the name of your Father." She just looked at me like I was from Mars. I did not dare look at her pastor.

"Just close your eyes," I instructed, "and let's see what happens. I am not going to sing in English, so you will not have to bother paying attention to the words." And I began.[1] After a couple of minutes I heard a sniff. I sneaked a quick look to see a tear rolling down her cheek and kept singing. In another minute she was crying profusely. In another minute she was crying strongly, which went on for the next six or seven minutes as I just kept singing. Finally she stopped crying and I stopped singing.

"Oh, that was wonderful!" she gushed.

"It was?" I almost replied. But what I said was, "Well, what happened?"

"I kept getting pictures of Jesus holding me when I was a baby and dancing with me at my birthday party and carrying me on His shoulders at a park and sitting on the edge of my bed while I slept and pushing chocolate pudding all over my mouth and"—she broke into profuse tears again. Tears of release, tears of healing.

In those few moments the Lord broke through her walls and began a life-changing healing. She still needed months of counseling and emotional healing, but she was no longer choked off by her painful past. He did all the work. My only job was to love. Did I *feel* like loving in that way? Of course not. We will get to that definition of love later in the chapter.

Love for God

A wonderful story of a love for God coming out of a sin-bruised heart is found in Luke 7. Jesus is dining at the home of a Pharisee when a sinful woman wets His feet with her tears, dries them with her hair and then pours perfume on them. Jesus commented on her act in depth, concluding, "I tell you, her many sins have been forgiven—for she loved much" (verse 47). Jesus seems to be saying that love preempts or cancels or triumphs over one's sins. Let me explain a cultural fact here. The feet are the lowest part of a person's body—lowest structurally but also socially. In Jesus' time, only the lowest slave ministered to a guest's feet. But a woman's hair was her glory. It was her crown. This woman took her glory to wipe the feet of Jesus. He called this much love.

May I encourage you to realize that He has paid off every single sin you have committed. And may I encourage you to express your gratitude with effusive love and with your glory.

An essential expression of love for God is worship. The Greek word *proskuneo* gives a good literal definition of what worship is: *pros*—toward; *kuneo*—to kiss. Thus, *proskuneo* means "to come toward to kiss." In other words, intimacy is what God wants from us. God directs us to worship Him because in worship we come into wonderful, loving closeness with Him, and He is what we need. I could not begin to guess the number of times the Spirit has washed over me in the midst of congregational worship. How wonderful it is that the last 25 years have brought a renewal of worship that has gone around the world. Most of this renewal is in song, for singing to God is the primary means of expressing intimacy.

I make a wisecrack about worship, saying, "If you do not like to worship, you are gonna have a heck of a time in heaven, 'cause that is all they do there." This is true. We must learn to worship effectively. For worship to be full, it must be done in the presence of others who also are worshiping. This means that love for God cannot be satisfactorily experienced apart from membership in His Church. Sometimes, what touches me in worship is the timbre of someone else's voice singing to

God. Or maybe knowing what has gone on in a worship leader's life. It can be the sound of a particular instrument. Often the fervor of love expressed to God warms me. None of this could take place by myself.

And worship brings us before the throne of God. It ushers us into His presence.

Some years after I began to practice the presence of God with my watch's countdown mechanism, checking in with Him every 24 minutes, I looked up the passages in the book of Revelation that mention those 24 elders who surround his throne:

> Whenever the living creatures give glory, honor and thanks to him who sits on the throne and who lives for ever and ever, the twenty-four elders fall down before him who sits on the throne, and worship him who lives for ever and ever. They lay their crowns before the throne and say: "You are worthy, our Lord and God, to receive glory and honor and power, for you created all things, and by your will they were created and have their being."
>
> . . . And when he had taken [the scroll], the four living creatures and the twenty-four elders fell down before the Lamb. Each one had a harp and they were holding golden bowls full of incense, which are the prayers of the saints. And they sang a new song: "You are worthy to take the scroll and to open its seals, for you were slain and with your blood you purchased men for God from every tribe and language and people and nation. You have made them to be a kingdom and priests to serve our God, and they will reign on the earth." . . .
>
> The four living creatures said, "Amen," and the elders fell down and worshiped.
>
> Revelation 4:9–11; 5:8–10, 14

I realized that the elders praise God for three things in particular. Those three things have given rich life to my love for God. They are creation, redemption and reign—ways in which God shows us His tremendous love for us.

Praise God for His Creation

What a creative genius God is! To call Him a genius is, of course, to apply a human title and is wholly inadequate, as He is so much more than human. But given my human inadequacy, "genius" still pops off my lips as I express my admiration to Him for creation. What an incredible Creator!

Each weekday I walk through farmlands as I pray for my list of concerns. What a God who makes crops grow! What genius is evident in their seed form, then seedling stage, then growth into mature fruits and vegetables for harvesting. It is miraculous! How marvelously different is cabbage from celery, expressed partly through the difference in their shades of green as you look across a field! I look up in one direction and see the mountains. What glory is a mountain! I look in the other direction and see the Channel Islands just a few miles off the coast. In my city our tree is the Hong Kong Coral. Have you seen these profligate red blossoms? They knock your eye out. What creation miracles do you boast in your area?

What huge creative genius went into conceptualizing and actualizing the sea! Some months ago my wife Sue and I were snorkeling while on vacation. What glories under the surface! What a God! The wonderful, splashy color schemes of tropical fish are delightful to admire. The way they pick at coral and dart through its crevices is entrancing. We stood in chest deep water to feed and pet stingrays. Have you ever felt the liquid velvet of a stingray's skin? It is amazing. Your fingers cannot get enough of it.

My wife called me on her cell phone yesterday to make sure I did not miss the sunset. It was worth the time.

Paul states that creation is evidence of God's existence: "His eternal power and divine nature . . . have been clearly seen, being understood from what has been made" (Romans 1:20). But creation is not just to convince us that He exists. It is a continuing gift to us—a gift of love. God wants us to enjoy this gift and relish Him for giving it.

I once taught on worship for seven consecutive weeks in my congregation and never repeated myself. The Scriptures are full of information on worship. Put the Psalms into your daily devotions and you will soon find nature prompting praise. There you will find heaven and earth, seas and mountains, birds and animals, winds and plants, sun and moon, grain and wine, incense and lips urging you to connect with, enjoy and worship the Creator. But do not just enjoy creation in the Book. Get out in it. In nature are lessons, promptings, assurances and delights that will direct you straight into conversation with God. I always take my monthly prayer days in the wild. Through creation God has told me much.

Let God talk to you through nature. Talk back to Him because of it.

Praise God for His Redemption

As great as creation is, even greater is His work of redemption. What a merciful God to have planned and pulled off the drama of salvation! When Adam and Eve sinned, the plan had already been long in effect: "He will crush your head, and you will strike his heel" (Genesis 3:15). The Lord said this about Jesus to the snake. Peter explains that we were redeemed "with the precious blood of Christ, a lamb without blemish or defect. He was chosen before the creation of the world" (1 Peter 1:19–20).

That the heart of the Father would be ripped apart through the staggering suffering of His own Son was a done deal before one speck of matter was created. That the Son agreed with that plan, foreknowing His pain, was part of that deal. In our church we sing a song with the line, "I'll never know how much it cost to see my sin upon that cross." We cannot imagine what it cost the Father and the Son to achieve our salvation. We can read about it and try to digest it, but we cannot put ourselves in Their places and experience what They experienced. On my walk the other day I recalled the thought expressed in Hebrews 6:4–6 and 10:29–31 that to keep on sinning is to crucify Jesus all over again and subject Him to public disgrace. I prayed, "Every time I sin I am lashing Your back, Lord Jesus," and I shuddered.

Many churches hold a three-hour service on Good Friday. These are a helpful way of reminding us what it cost the Trinity to redeem us. In the Garden of Gethsemane Jesus experienced *hematidrosis*, bleeding sweat. Shocking emotional stress produces the breaking of tiny capillaries in the sweat glands, mixing blood with perspiration. Next, the crown of thorns was fashioned to mock His claim to kingship. Then He was tried in court—several times! Next came the scourging with 39 lashes made of leather embedded with shards of steel and bone that had killed a number of criminals outright.

Duane Spencer put it this way:

> His entire body would at last be an unrecognizable mass of torn tissue matted with blood and serum. . . . Throwing His own raiment over His half-swooning body, the Roman Soldiers next forced Him to shoulder the crossbeam to which He should be nailed. The flesh was so weakened by now through emotional exhaustion and loss of blood that the dear Lord Jesus staggered under the load. The crossbeam (sometimes weighing over 100 pounds) was too much, so they pressed a stranger from Cyrene into service. . . .
>
> Once at the site of the crucifixion our Lord would have been forced to lie flat on the ground with His arms stretched apart above His head. Taking a rough, square spike, the centurion on duty would have then driven it through His wrist into the crossbeam. The second crude nail would follow into the other wrist. . . .
>
> Fixed firmly in place by the cruel nails, the limp form of Jesus would be hauled by the crossbeam up the pole. . . . Again the searching thumb of the centurion would feel for the indentation between bones, and the long spike would be hammered through His feet into the wood beneath.

The excruciating agony of the spike burning through the nerves between the metatarsal bones of the feet jerk the body of the Saviour erect, only to have the leg muscles convulse and drive His body downward. This places body weight on the wrist nails so that the flaming pain explodes in the brain of the Victim as the median nerves shriek their signal of torment. Then, as the muscles of the arms and legs show fatigue, an awful series of spasms cramp Him in positions which make the drawing of breath more difficult. Suffocation drives desperate muscles into action as the gibbeted One strives for oxygen. Then, in the midst of the muscle-tearing convulsions and the sucking in of air which cannot be exhaled until the build-up of carbon dioxide in the lungs and blood stream relieve the cramps, the glorious Son of God speaks to those about Him! (Then He gives the seven sayings from the cross.)

Then, after having endured hours and hours of unbelievable torture, the final agonies prophetically described in the 22nd Psalm begin to set in. The compressed heart pumps the sluggish, thickening blood into the tissues, becoming like wax melting down into the midst of the bowels. The awful shock to the heart by the locking-cramps, and its constriction by the fluid in the pericardium, blends the watery fluid of the heart sac and the heavy blood from its interior. Having given up His pure Spirit to the Father, at His own will, the Lord Jesus dies. His work on behalf of sinners is finished.[2]

That is more data than you wanted to read, isn't it? And it represents only the *physical* dynamics that were occurring. The *spiritual* aspects are as profound: "God made him who had no sin to be sin for us, so that in him we might become the righteousness of God" (2 Corinthians 5:21). In other words, all the sins of all mankind were somehow compressed into a spear that the Father drove into the soul of His Son. Jesus not only bore our sins, but He became sin itself. And sin itself was judged, punished and executed in the Person of the Son of God on that cross. A just God could do no less than to fully judge, punish and execute sin. It was His mercy that drove Him to accomplish all this in the body and soul of His own Son.

A song I frequently find on my lips during my morning walk is this:

Hallelujah, My Father,
For giving us Your Son,
Sending Him into the world
To be given up for man,
Knowing we would bruise Him
And smite Him from the earth.
Hallelujah, my Father,
In His death is my birth.
Hallelujah, my Father,
In His life is my life.[3]

Praise God for redemption! Praise Him for what it cost Him! Praise Him for its benefits to you!

Praise God for His Reign

The third quality for which the 24 elders praise God is His reign. He is the King. He reigns. We live and move and have our being under His rulership—and He is a good, just and loving King.

I wish I could take you on a tour of some developing countries that have not yet had much experience of the reign of God, being ruled instead by gods that are not He. You would be prompted to praise Him for His goodness to you. In America, we are extremely fortunate. The influence of God on the foundation of Western culture continues to bear magnificent benefits to those who live in it. We take that reign for granted.

But there are many places on this earth where that reign has not been established. And you can see the difference in politics, economy, social life, physical health and relational well-being. We have every reason to praise God for His munificence toward us.

I could write a book on the blessings that have come to me by virtue of establishing Jesus as Lord over my life. I now laugh at my reluctance early in my spiritual life to turn over lordship to Him. I was foolish to think I could run my own life. He has enriched every area that I turned over to Him. He has solved every problem. He has blessed every relationship. He has enlarged every opportunity. He has expanded every resource. He has banished every sorrow. He has even healed almost every illness. So I praise Him for His reign, His kingship, His capabilities, His wisdom and His mercy.

He indeed knows how to reign. Part of my job is to install Jesus as King wherever I go, for every place needs His reign and I need it in every place. And when I see how He has reigned, it provokes praises from my heart and my lips. He is a gracious King.

☙ Love for Self

Jesus' summary of the law included, "Love your neighbor as yourself" (Matthew 22:39; Mark 12:31; Galatians 5:14). The implication is that you are going to love yourself. Sometimes this is not so easy.

Mike Scanlan, a Catholic priest in the healing movement, says that our hearts may need to be healed before we can love ourselves. He notes that heart healing is needed when a person has:

1. a judgmental spirit that is hard on self and others;
2. a strong perfectionist attitude demanding the impossible of self and others;
3. a pattern of fearing future events;
4. a sense of aloneness and abandonment in times of decision;
5. a preoccupation with one's own guilt;
6. and a compulsion to compete with others for position and success.

Overarching all of these things is self-rejection. When you reject yourself for something, that something stands out in other people's eyes like a green wart on a yellow nose. But when you accept yourself, that thing slips out of other people's minds. Your own displeasure with it is what triggers *their* awareness of it.

If I hate myself—whether it is for being tall, or short, or blond, or brunette, or male, or female, or white, or black, or clumsy, or alcoholic, or sick, or an only child, or tongue-tied, or unresponsive, or anxious, or fat, or thin, or plain or immature—then others are going to notice those very things about me. But if I have dealt with those things in the grace of God, then others do not notice them at all—or if they do, they think well of them.

The cure involves several roles.

1. *The role of God.* This is foundational. He is the One who sets the foundation, the rock, on which you stand to accept yourself. And that Rock is Jesus.

2. *The role of the Bible.* This is revelatory. The Bible tells me the basis for the acceptance of myself by God, by others and by myself.

And that basis is Jesus Himself. "He hath made us accepted in the beloved," Paul asserts in Ephesians 1:6 (KJV). I cannot accept you for yourself. I can accept you only in Christ Jesus. I can accept *me* only in Christ Jesus. Because He is fully acceptable, so are you, and so am I. My wife, Sue, says it this way: "I can accept you when I like you or what you are doing. It is when I do not like you or your action that I have to call upon Jesus to give me His love to accept you." And she has done it many times.

Listening prayer is also helpful here. So is replacing negative thoughts with God-thoughts. We must learn to counter negative self-talk with positive, scriptural self-talk.

3. *The role of others.* This is essential. When you see me for who I am and accept me anyway, it enables me to begin to accept myself. If you have not spilled the beans about yourself, you do not know if others really accept you, because you do

not *know* if they would accept you if they knew the truth about you. That keeps you from believing that God accepts you and that you can accept you.

4. *The role of faith.* This is willful. I have been saying this all through this book. At first, we just make the decision to accept and love ourselves. C. S. Lewis says, "God loves us; not because we are lovable but because He is love, not because He needs to receive but because He delights to give."[4]

5. *The role of you.* This is appropriation. This is receiving. It is a work of faith. "Your job is to believe," Jesus said (see John 6:29).

This will take time. It is a process. Some things have to change before other things can change. Various factors may have to come into play at certain points: inner healing, deliverance, teaching and expressed forgiveness. But self-acceptance and self-love are foundational to success, happiness, usefulness, relationships and ministry, so they must be attained.

Once you love yourself, you can much more effectively turn your love toward others. The following statements by George MacDonald bring self-love into focus through appropriating God's love for us.

- Thou wilt care for me with Thy perfect fatherhood.
- Help is always within God's reach when His children want it.
- It is hard on God when His children will not let Him give—when they carry themselves so that He must withhold His hand lest He harm them.
- He who is made in the image of God must know Him or be desolate: The child must have the Father!
- What if He knows prayer to be the thing we need first and most? Communion with God is the one need of the soul beyond all other needs.
- To bring His child to His knee, God withholds that man may ask.

- The prayer, far more than the opportunity of answering it, is God's end.

- The best argument that He has help is that we have need.

- To talk with God is more than to have all prayers granted.

- Whatever serves to clear any difficulty from the way of the recognition of the Father will more or less undermine every difficulty in life.[5]

Love for Others

Earlier I mentioned that Jesus took 614 laws and reduced them to two. His followers further reduced them to one. Paul, for example, says, "The entire law is summed up in a single command: 'Love your neighbor as yourself'" (Galatians 5:14). In Romans 13:8 he says much the same: "He who loves his fellowman has fulfilled the law." Two verses later he repeats, "Therefore love is the fulfillment of the law."

James implies the same thing when he says, "If you really keep the royal law found in Scripture, 'Love your neighbor as yourself,' you are doing right" (2:8). The apostle John says it like this, "If we love one another, God lives in us and his love is made complete in us" (1 John 4:12).

I am not canceling what I said about loving God. But if you love God and express your love for Him, you will soon find yourself confronted with the requirement to love others for whom He paid the ultimate price. If you love Him and He loves them, then you have to love them, too.

This brings us back to the matter of will. When feelings of love come on their own—Hallelujah!—that is a gift. But when they do not, you are supposed to love anyway. In such instances, loving is an act of will. And what the will does is make decisions. Years ago our congregation's couples profited from a video series entitled "Love Is a Decision."[6] The title itself blessed them, for many had brought to the course an unexamined assumption that love was a feeling and that feeling was outside of one's control. Feelings are beyond our direct governable control, but love is not. You behave lovingly, and feelings eventually find their way in support of the behavior. A short way to say it is that decision releases effect. Or feelings follow faith.

But what kind of love? Here is a comparison of two kinds of love, using the Greek words:

Eros (human)	*Agape* (divine)
What can you do for me?	What can I do for you?
Self-centered	Other centered
Based in and expressed through feelings	Based in and expressed through will
Hold on to your life and lose it	Lose your life for My sake and gain it
Conditional	Unconditional
Immature	Mature
Self-satisfying	Self-giving
Unstable foundation for relationships	Stable foundation for relationships
Limited	Unlimited

The challenge is to love with *agape* love. Remember the promise "Love never fails" (1 Corinthians 13:8)? Each person has a longing deep inside just to be loved, warts and all. Most of the unacceptable behavior in which people engage is because they do not really believe they are truly loved just as they are. So they try to test that love or provoke it or earn it or reject it.

But an astonishing thing happens when they know deep inside that they are loved: They straighten out. When those around them give up trying to change them and just love them as they are, they tend to straighten out, get their acts together and mellow out. When God tells us in Scripture to love with *agape* love, He is launching us on the greatest adventure we can experience, for He is telling us to do the same thing He does.

God desperately wants people to change. He wants us to stop hurting each other, to help each other, to be a blessing instead of a curse to others. But He gives us the rewards for change before we change one single thing. We get an "A" for the whole course on the first day of the course. He bathes us in unconditional love every second of every day. God says, "I am going to love you totally whether you end up improving in this life or not." When we realize that He truly loves us like that, it just melts our hearts and we end up changing for the best of reasons—because we want to, not because we have to.

God wants to express that quality of love through you to others, for He is an incarnationalist up to His hairline. That big word just means that He insists on disclosing Himself through human beings like you. If you love, He is revealed.

Listen to this challenge by Emmet Fox:

> There is no difficulty that enough love will not conquer; no disease that enough love will not heal; no door that enough love will not open; no gulf that enough love will not bridge; no wall that enough love will not throw down; no sin that enough love will not redeem. It makes no difference how deeply seated may be the trouble, how hopeless the outlook, how muddled the tangle, how great the mistake: a sufficient realization of love will dissolve it all. . . . If only you could love enough you would be the happiest and most powerful being in the world.[7]

That last phrase is intriguing. It brings before us a choice to love with *eros* or *agape*. Eros I can do on my own. But *agape* is going to require God helping me. *Eros* will dismiss Fox's challenge as nonsense. *Agape* will take it on. Here's what I have found so far: I am not yet loving others with that quality of *agape* love, but the repeated attempt has made me happier than I could have imagined.

Love like Jesus

Let's get back to Jesus. He stated clearly: "If you love me, obey my commandments." "My command is this: Love each other as I have loved you" (John 14:15; 15:12). Jesus loves with self-giving, self-sacrificing love. He is the model for how we are to love. If you love like Him, you will be blessed even if nobody else changes. But He guarantees that if we love like Him, great changes will be loosed upon mankind: "Love never fails."

Love the Poor

One category of people Jesus loved profusely is the poor (Matthew 11:5; 19:21; Mark 10:21; 12:42–44; Luke 4:18; 6:20; 7:22; 14:13–14, 21; 16:19–31; 18:22; 21:2–4). And the Old Testament teaches, "He who is kind to the poor lends to the LORD, and he will reward him for what he has done" (Proverbs 19:17).

I can personally testify to many rewards for having tried to minister to the poor. One fellow the Lord brought into our home had come to Southern California on a vendetta. He had spent all his money tracking down the man who had raped his daughter. Finally he trapped him in his garage and wound a garrote around his neck. But having finally gotten the man in his hands, he found that he could not go through with it and let him go. He stumbled into my church office and poured out the story. I checked with Jesus, who nodded that we should take him into our home. Late one night, after having spent several days with us, he gave his life to Jesus. All we did was house, feed and listen to him for a few days. What a cheap price to pay for a man's eternal salvation.

Another who had been in Leavenworth many years for murder surrendered to Jesus in our living room. Another demanded to be baptized in our kitchen sink at midnight. Another was overheard laughing scornfully at our testimony as he lay on our bed in the guest room. Another was arrested by the police in our family room. Another tried to push our car out of the driveway to hotwire it. Another ended up in a mental hospital—twice. I could go on. None of these persons was able to repay us for having taken them into our home. But God repaid us abundantly in blessings, protection, money and much more.

Our church engaged the six categories of poor whom Jesus identifies as Himself in Matthew 25: strangers, naked, hungry, sick, imprisoned and thirsty. We had programs for each type of need. God's response was to bless *every other aspect* of our church's life. We never had money problems. In fact, we did nothing to raise money; God handled it. We were remarkably united; there was almost no strife among our people. Our missions—we did 150 of them in ten years—were blessed with much favor, power and good effect. Our buildings remained unscathed by graffiti and earthquakes. We just did what Jesus told us to do and He handled all the rest. May I encourage you to talk with your church about ministering to the poor?

"If anyone has material possessions and sees his brother in need but has no pity on him, how can the love of God be in him? Dear children, let us not love with words or tongue but with actions and in truth" (1 John 3:17–18).

And to quote George MacDonald again: "We shall never be able, I say, to rest in the bosom of the Father, until His *father-hood* is fully revealed to us in the love of the brothers. For He cannot be our father save as He is their father; and if we do not see Him and feel Him as their father, we cannot know Him as ours."[8]

Love for Enemies

Remember my story in chapter 6 in which the Lord challenged me to fast and pray for an enemy? That was something I—did—not—want—to—do! But the blessings that have come to me through that experience have been staggering. What glories I would have missed had I refused. What power I would have foregone, what tenderness I would have never seen, what faith in God I would have missed, what knowledge of His heart

175

I would have skipped! When you pour hot water through a pipe, the pipe gets warm first. I thank God for that whole episode, for I can write to you from a heart of experience and not just a theory that love for enemies works.

Who is your enemy? Will you accept the challenge to love that person? Jesus said, "If you love those who love you, what credit is that to you? Even 'sinners' love those who love them. . . . But love your enemies, do good to them, and lend to them without expecting to get anything back. Then your reward will be great, and you will be sons of the Most High, because he is kind to the ungrateful and wicked" (Luke 6:32, 35). Matthew's version of this passage adds that we are to pray for our enemies (see 5:44). Love, do good to, lend to, pray for—these are heavy things to do for an enemy. But God wants the Christian world to do these things for enemies! Nothing could testify more strongly about the character of Jesus.

If Jesus says, "Your reward will be great" (Luke 6:35), it must be a pretty spectacular reward. He does not use the word "great" very often. But love for enemies brings it into use. Inversely, "But whoever hates his brother is in the darkness and walks around in the darkness; he does not know where he is going, because the darkness has blinded him" (1 John 2:11). Walk blinded or walk in great reward. That is the choice. Choose love.

9

"Your Goodness Proves Mine"

I am convinced that the seven commands we have studied are crucial for the health not only of each of us personally but also of our cities, our nations and the entire world—as well as the Kingdom of God. The problem with the world is its poor assimilation of Christianity. The problem with Christianity is its poor assimilation of Christ. The Church and the world are in great need of Jesus Himself. And He has made the potentially catastrophic or glorious decision to disclose Himself primarily through the likes of you and me. His goodness, therefore, is manifested in us.

Grow Up into His Goodness

In order to serve as a true reflection of who He is, we must grow up into His goodness. I have never heard anyone preach on the following passage in the book of Hebrews, which I believe is obscure because so few address it:

We have much to say about this, but it is hard to explain because you are slow to learn. In fact, though by this time you ought to be teachers, you need someone to teach you the elementary truths of God's word all over again. You need milk, not solid food! Anyone who lives on milk, being still an infant, is not acquainted with the teaching about righteousness. But solid food is for the mature, who by constant use have trained themselves to distinguish good from evil. Therefore let us leave the elementary teachings about Christ and go on to maturity, not laying again the foundation of repentance from acts that lead to death, and of faith in God, instruction about baptisms, the laying on of hands, the resurrection of the dead, and eternal judgment. And God permitting, we will do so.

Hebrews 5:11–6:3

This passage signals for us a momentous truth: God expects us to grow up. I would not be able to count how many times I have preached on what this passage calls the "elementary truths": repentance, faith, baptisms, laying on of hands, resurrection and judgment. The writer calls all this baby food.

Perhaps, then, a steak would be straightforward obedience to Jesus' top seven commands.

Reward and Punishment Revisited

Jesus' Sermon on the Mount (Matthew 5–7) is His most famous teaching. It is a directive sermon. The thrust of the Beatitudes is that you will be blessed if you *do* such and such. "Do" and "do not" occur frequently. The repeated phrase "It has been said . . . but I say to you" signals Jesus' reinterpretation of the law for us.

The top seven commands that are the focus of this book all are referenced in the Sermon on the Mount. Let's quickly review these.

1. Love—"Love your enemies and pray for those who perse-cute you, that you may be sons of your Father in heaven" (Matthew 5:44–45).
2. Believe—"If that is how God clothes the grass of the field, which is here today and tomorrow is thrown into the fire, will he not much more clothe you, O you of little faith?" (6:30).
3. Forgive—"If you do not forgive men their sins, your Father will not forgive your sins" (6:15).
4. Watch—"Watch out for false prophets. . . . By their fruit you will recognize them" (7:15–16).
5. Give—"But when you give to the needy, do not let your left hand know what your right hand is doing, so that your giving may be in secret. Then your Father, who sees what is done in secret, will reward you" (6:3–4).
6. Grow Up—"But seek first his kingdom and his righ-teousness, and all these things will be given to you as well" (6:33).
7. Hear—"Everyone who hears these words of mine and puts them into practice is like a wise man who built his house on the rock" (7:24).

Jesus concludes the Sermon on the Mount with the com-parison of wise and foolish builders:

Therefore everyone who hears these words of mine and *puts them into practice* is like a wise man who built his house on the rock. The rain came down, the streams rose, and the winds blew and beat against that house; yet it did not fall, because it had its foundation on the rock. But everyone who hears these words of mine and *does not put them into practice* is like a fool-ish man who built his house on sand. The rain came down, the streams rose, and the winds blew and beat against that house, and it fell with a great crash.

Matthew 7:24–27

Jesus claims—and our lives affirm—that the rains will come down, the streams will rise and the winds will blow and beat against our houses. Times of testing will come. The difference is how ready we are for them. Wisdom is obeying Jesus; foolishness is disobeying Him.

In this most famous teaching Jesus uses the word *reward* nine times. This suggests that there also will be a punishment for those who disobey. Psalm 98:9 predicts, "[The LORD] comes to judge the earth. He will judge the world in righteousness and the peoples with equity." Revelation 21:6–8 compares the obedient and the disobedient in judgment:

> He said to me: "It is done. I am the Alpha and the Omega, the Beginning and the End. To him who is thirsty I will give to drink without cost from the spring of the water of life. He who overcomes will inherit all this, and I will be his God and he will be my son. But the cowardly, the unbelieving, the vile, the murderers, the sexually immoral, those who practice magic arts, the idolaters and all liars—their place will be in the fiery lake of burning sulfur."

Perhaps we should ask the question: How far do you have to go with God to "overcome"? This passage clearly indicates that our personal lives will be judged and that we will face either a reward or a punishment according to our obedience.

Toward the end of His earthly ministry, Jesus spoke of trying times and concluded, "But he who stands firm to the end will be saved" (Matthew 24:13). The implication is that those who do not stand firm will not be saved. He may be suggesting that one can be a believer and not make it because of copping out under testing. How about Judas, who betrayed Jesus? Was he ever a true believer? I suspect he was. Hebrews 6 speaks of those who have truly believed but have fallen away:

> It is impossible for those who have once been enlightened, who have tasted the heavenly gift, who have shared in the Holy Spirit, who have tasted the goodness of the word of God and

the powers of the coming age, if they fall away, to be brought back to repentance, because to their loss they are crucifying the Son of God all over again and subjecting him to public disgrace.

Land that drinks in the rain often falling on it and that produces a crop useful to those for whom it is farmed receives the blessing of God. But land that produces thorns and thistles is worthless and is in danger of being cursed. In the end it will be burned.

Hebrews 6:4–8

Revelation 22:12 begins the last paragraph of the Bible that is spoken by Jesus: "Behold, I am coming soon! My reward is with me, and I will give to everyone according to what he has done." Paul mentioned similar judgments about thirty years before Revelation was written:

For of this you can be sure: No immoral, impure or greedy person—such a man is an idolater—has any inheritance in the kingdom of Christ and of God. Let no one deceive you with empty words, for because of such things God's wrath comes on those who are disobedient.

Ephesians 5:5–6

The New Testament suggests a minimum of three kinds of postdeath people: the damned, the saved and the rewarded. In His fairness, God will put each of us precisely where our faith and our works determine we should be.

In one of those pearly gates stories, a rich churchgoer is met by St. Peter, who tells her he is taking her to her heavenly abode. They enter the heavenly Beverly Hills and she begins to hope that one of these mansions is hers. But they pass through without stopping. The same happens with several more upscale neighborhoods, then a middle-class area, then an impoverished region. Finally, St. Peter stops in front of a one-room hovel and beckons for the woman to enter.

"Why, I couldn't possibly spend two minutes in there, not to mention all eternity!" she exclaims. With a look and gesture of great sadness, St. Peter gently says, "But my dear, this is the best we could do with the materials you sent up."

It is easy to judge such a person. But there must be no gloating in successful obedience, and no judging of others for disobedience. That would displease the Lord, for love "thinks no evil."

Tension between Salvation and Obedience

The relationship between salvation and obedience brings us right back to the tension we looked at in chapter 1. It can be stated several ways:

justification by faith alone	yet	faith without works is dead
grow in the reception and digestion of grace	while	displaying that grace in being and doing
punishment	or	reward
fear not	and	fear
confess sins and get forgiven	but	get enough grace to stop sinning
getting into heaven is by grace	and	where you end up in heaven is by works
believe	then	obey
get saved	and	act saved
plead for mercy	and	act in thanks for mercy received

A priest in New York was called to a house of prostitution. An old man, coming down the stairs, had been struck with a heart attack. The priest sat beside him on the stairs and assessed that his situation was critical. "Are you sorry for your sins?" he asked the man.

"No, Father, I can't honestly say that I am."

"Do you want to be sorry for your sins?"

"Hmmm, no I can't be honest and say that either."

"Do you want *to want* to be sorry for your sins?"

"Yes, Father, I want to want to be sorry for them."

So the priest pronounced absolution, asking God to forgive the man of his sins. Then the man died. This story describes the lengths mercy will go to achieve its purposes. But it leaves us with questions: Where would he have ended up if he did not believe in Jesus? In hell. Where did he end up, having confessed faith in Jesus? In heaven. Was he happy there? Well, the mercy of God had gotten him out of hell, but he surely did not receive the reward God wanted him to have. He was saved, but his level of obedience—or lack thereof—determined the level of his reward.

The Way to Reward

God is crafty. It takes obedience to the top seven commands to get rewarded, but it takes Jesus to obey the top seven commands. You cannot satisfactorily obey them by yourself. But you are expected to try with all your might.

Someone asked Jesus, "'Lord, are only a few people going to be saved?' He said to them, 'Make every effort to enter through the narrow door, because many, I tell you, will try to enter and will not be able to. Once the owner of the house gets up and closes the door, you will stand outside knocking and pleading, "Sir, open the door for us." But he will answer, "I don't know you or where you come from."'" The Amplified Bible puts it: "Strive to enter by the narrow door—force yourselves through it—for many, I tell you, will try to enter and will not be able" (Luke 13:23–25).

This recalls Matthew 11:12, where Jesus said, "From the days of John the Baptist until now, the kingdom of heaven has been forcefully advancing, and forceful men lay hold of it." Again, the Amplified Bible says, "And violent men seize it by force [as a precious prize]—a share in the heavenly kingdom is sought for with most ardent zeal and intense exertion."

Make every effort. . . . Force yourselves through it. . . . Forceful men lay hold of it. . . . Sought for with most ardent zeal and intense

183

exertion. These are not laid-back attitudes or behaviors. This is not the realm of the sophisticate or dilettante. These are not the attitudes of the confident or the unconcerned.

The word *strive* is *agonizesthe* in the Greek, from which we get the word *agonize*.

Make every effort, strive, force yourselves, agonize—these are the attitudes of the desperate. These are the goals of the utterly determined. This is the orientation of those who have seen the prize and decided that it is worth any price.

Seeking Jesus First—Everything Is Worth Sacrificing for It

One way to "strive" is to keep short- and long-term goals clear. The right relationship between daily and eternal needs is summed up in Matthew 6:33: "But seek first his kingdom and his righteousness, and all these things will be given to you as well."

The Kingdom comes first, daily needs second. But we sometimes get into the reverse mind-set: "Lord, just let me get my needs straightened out, and then I will pursue You with great energy." We act as though the pursuit of God is something that can be done with leftover energy. We say to Jesus: first a roof, then a job, next a car, then a few new clothes and finally I would like to get a little cushion in the bank, *then* I will be able to afford to seek You with all my heart. But Jesus says: *Look, seek Me first with all your heart; then I will take care of house and car and job and clothes and recreation and all your other needs.*

Great hordes of people are not even trying to get in the narrow door. And Jesus says that not everyone who tries will be able to get through it. Why? Because they are not trying or they have waited too long to begin trying, or they have not tried enough yet to realize that they must have His help.

Did Paul ever think that he had it made? He said to the Corinthians:

Everyone who competes in the games goes into strict training. They do it to get a crown that will not last; but we do it to get a crown that will last forever. Therefore I do not run like a man running aimlessly; I do not fight like a man beating the air. No, I beat my body and make it my slave so that after I have preached to others, *I myself will not be disqualified for the prize.*

1 Corinthians 9:25–27

This was written about A.D. 55. Note that he expresses the possibility of losing out on the prize.

Six years later, he said to the Philippians:

Not that I have already obtained all this, or have already been made perfect, but I press on to take hold of that for which Christ Jesus took hold of me. Brothers, I do not consider myself yet to have taken hold of it. But one thing I do: Forgetting what is behind and straining toward what is ahead, I press on toward the goal to win the prize for which God has called me heavenward in Christ Jesus.

Philippians 3:12–14

By this time Paul had been a follower of Jesus for about 25 years, and yet here he states his intent to keep at this business of pursuing Christ and His reward.

Four or five years after that, in the last year of his life, he told Timothy:

For I am already being poured out like a drink offering, and the time has come for my departure. I have fought the good fight, I have finished the race, *I have kept the faith.* Now there is in store for me the crown of righteousness, which the Lord, the righteous Judge, will award to me on that day—and not only to me, but also to all who have longed for his appearing.

2 Timothy 4:6–8

So eventually Paul did think he had it made, but only at the very end of his life, after following Jesus with all his heart for thirty years. Paul took the narrow door. He sought Jesus first.

Taking the Narrow Door

What about *us*? What does it require to take Jesus radically seriously? To force ourselves through the narrow door?

First, it takes caring more for God than anything else. One must use one's will to overcome the things that compete with God for allegiance.

Second, we must keep short accounts. We need to confess as soon as we mess up; we cannot wait until Sunday. And sometimes this can be embarrassing. One Tuesday I drove 75 miles up to the top of Mt. Evans, behind Denver, for a time of listening to the Lord. He reminded me that a few days earlier I had acted brusquely toward a clerk at CompUSA. *Go apologize to her* was His only message to me that day. So I drove all the way back to Denver and apologized to the woman. But do you know what? I am glad I obeyed Him, for my obedience freed His voice to come to me once again, and it freed me to enjoy His presence.

Third, forcing ourselves through the narrow door means working at obeying God. George MacDonald asks, "Do you want to live by faith? Do you want to know Christ aright? Do you want to awake and arise and *live*, but do not know how? I will tell you: Get up, and do something the Master tells you. The moment you do, you instantly make yourself His disciple. Instead of asking yourself whether you believe or not, ask yourself if you have this day done one single thing because He said, 'Do it,' or once abstained because He said, 'Do not do it.'. . . It is simply absurd to say you believe, or even want to believe in Him, if you do not do anything He tells you."[1] You will find that just doing something Jesus tells you results in blessing. It resolves conflicts, solves problems, fills needs and adds to the fullness of life. If you summon your courage and your will, you will be able to do many of the things He tells you to do. But there will be some that you are unable to do.

That is when it takes a fourth thing, as I have hinted: It takes more Jesus in you. Paul used the two words "in Christ" over eighty times in his letters. That is what it takes: being in Christ. This is because only Jesus can fully live the life of Jesus.

Collaborating with Jesus

How does this collaboration occur? The answer entails seven points, some of which are review, but some of which is anticipation.

First, we must recognize the importance of obeying Jesus.

Second, we must find out what His commands are.

Third, we have got to do what He tells us.

Fourth, we must come to the end of our ability to obey Him—a different experience for each of us.

Fifth, we must grab hold of His ability to obey in us.

Sixth, we must experiment with that collaboration, growing in our ability to let Him express Himself through us.

Seventh, we should rejoice at the wonders He accomplishes through us.

I would like to expand on this collaboration. It takes Jesus helping us at points one, two and three. If He does not help us, we will not become aware of the importance of obeying Him, nor will we find out what His commands are, and we certainly will not get it together to start actually obeying Him. But if we do all of this, after we have obeyed Him for a while our capacity for Him runs out and we cannot seem to go forward with new obedience. This is where point four comes in: coming to the end of our ability to obey Him. At this point His help is vital. It is an important crisis, for we either will start receding or we will find a way to appropriate His help and continue in obedience.

Coming to the End of Our Ability to Obey

Point four comes at different times and ages for each of us, but it does come to all of us. Many of us become somewhat aware that we are facing a blockage or pause in our growth in Christ. Often what we do is apply harder what has worked in the past. Or we regard it as spiritual warfare and press against it. Or we go on going on, because perseverance has helped in the past. All of these are reasonable courses of action.

But a new breakthrough still eludes us. We might even be ambushed by an old temptation and momentarily succumb to it. If so, we do what we have learned in the past: repent quickly, claim forgiveness and get back into the lap of Jesus. But that is just a stall. This procedure has not gotten us into the new . . . what? What should we call it? What is this thing that we are now aware we need but still eludes us? We do not know. We are not sure what we need. Past answers do not seem to work now. We are edgy, off center. We are still being useful to the Kingdom and still committed to its expansion, but something is . . . not exactly wrong, but something is missing.

Finally the Lord helps us. He was willing to help us all along, but we were not yet receptive to it. Somehow, someway He tells us that it is not something we need but Someone. He Himself. But more of Him.

I personally have hit this breakthrough several times at successive levels. About 26 years ago I discovered the book *They Found the Secret* by V. Raymond Edman, which tells of twenty leaders who ran into point four. The book describes how the Lord and they resolved the crisis. For each of them, the answer was more Jesus. I identified with two or three of these leaders in particular, for their stories or their personalities or their situations were similar to mine. Hudson Taylor's statement helped me immensely:

> The sweetest part, if one may speak of one part being sweeter than another, is the rest which full identification with Christ

brings. I am no longer anxious about anything, as I realize this; for He, I know, is able to carry out His will, and His will is mine. It makes no matter where He places me, or how. That is rather for Him to consider than for me; for in the easiest positions He must give me His grace, and in the most difficult His grace is sufficient.[2]

Edman quotes a contemporary of Taylor a few lines later: "He was an object lesson in quietness. He drew from the Bank of Heaven every farthing of his daily income—'My peace I give unto you.' Whatever did not agitate the Savior, or ruffle His spirit was not to agitate him."[3]

Ian Thomas's experience later in the book was my story. After struggling at point four for seven years, he had a breakthrough. Thomas writes it was as though the Lord was saying:

You see, for seven years, with utmost sincerity, you have been trying to live *for* Me, on My behalf, the life that I have been waiting for seven years to live *through* you. I have been there the whole time. All the things you have been pleading for, all the things for which you have been asking, have been yours since the day seven years ago, at your request and invitation, I came into your heart at the Crusader boys' camp; but you see, although you have given mental consent to the truth that I have been in your heart, and have accepted it as a theory, you have lived totally ignoring *the fact.* You have been busy trying to do *for* Me all that only I can do *through* you. Now supposing that I am your life and you begin to accept it as a fact, then I am your strength! You have been pleading and begging for that for seven years. I *am* your victory in every area of your life, if you want it![4]

Those words were gold to me, and I took them to the bank. I have drawn from that bank many times over the years. Through them the Lord took me into stage five, which quickly propelled me into stage six.

A funny pattern began to emerge after a decade or so: I was more useful but less capable. Another way to say it is that the Lord became more and more capable in me, through me.

As I mentioned earlier, a moment of revelation came one day through the words of Norman Grubb: "The goal in life is not to *be* somebody but to *contain* Someone."[5] My testimony is that as I have sought to contain and give forth Jesus, He mobilizes the best of me and brings me along in the deal.

This is a clear example of losing one's life and gaining it, as Jesus exhorted. To stop trying to be somebody is to lose your life. To start trying to contain Someone is to lose your life. But He is so good and kind that He sees to it that you experience richer and richer fullness for having made that decision.

One day I was in New Zealand leading a conference. The worship team sang a song that was new to me. One line of that song pierced my heart: "I need You more today than yesterday." Instantly I realized that on some unconscious level I had been expecting that as I grew in grace I would need the Lord less and less. This line nailed me. I repented instantly and like a child leaped back into the lap of my Boss, my Enabler, my Friend, my Jesus.

Grabbing Hold of His Ability to Obey in Us

How do you do point five? I do not know. I think He does it for us. But somehow we grab onto His ability to express more of Himself through us. I know that timing is crucial. One does not *decide* to come to the end of himself. You have to try and try until you exhaust your capabilities. Then, by grace, you *realize* that you have come to the end of yourself. That is when you can do stage five. MacDonald helps us see that the Lord has to wait until we are ready for more:

His children are not His real, true sons and daughters until they think like Him, feel with Him, judge as He judges, are at home with Him and without fear before Him because He and they mean the same thing, love the same things, seek the same ends.

He is our Father all the time, for He is true; but until we respond with the truth of children, He cannot let all the Father out to us; there is no place for the dove of His tenderness to alight. . . . Because we are His children, we must become His sons and daughters. Nothing will satisfy Him or do for us, but that we be one with our Father!

When God can do what He will with a man, the man may do what He will with the world.[6]

Thus, there are things God cannot say to me until I am ready for them. There are challenges that would swamp me until I have grown to their level by having met easier challenges. There are changes in the heart that prevent my hearing certain words of Jesus until those changes occur. There are truths that do not make sense until their more foundational truths have been *lived*.

Letting Him Express Himself through Us

Point six then becomes a glorious adventure. By His mercy we go from strength to strength. We go from one challenge to another, usually with wonderful results. We go from blessing to blessing. What a ride! What fun! What meaning!

Rejoicing at the Wonders He Accomplishes through Us

Point seven is a series of exultances. I do not mean to say that we do not have problems, challenges and obstacles to surmount. But a confidence born of past successes plants us firmly on the Rock, and we go forward in a peace that only He can give.

Years ago I bought a picture of Jesus and mounted it on the wall of my office. I taped a slip of paper to the bottom of the picture that read: "Because You must, You shall, and I will rest in that." Whatever needed doing, He had to do it, and I could relax about it. As challenges came, I looked at that picture and its promise time after time, year after year. Just in the last few months, the Lord has added to the statement. It now reads: "Because You must, You shall, and I will rest in that. Because *I* must, You shall, and I will rest in *that*." The newer version expresses a deeper partnership between Him and me.

At this stage of collaboration with Jesus, the truth of 1 John 5:3 becomes our experience: "This is love for God: to obey his commands. And his commandments are not burdensome." By His wonderfully and carefully executed program in us, we come to the place where His love and His commands are delightful rather than burdensome. I still yak at Him sometimes when He says to do something I would rather not, but we both know I am probably going to do it, and that it will turn out for my benefit as well as those He wants me to serve. Most of the time, it is just sheer excitement to know His love and offer it to others.

I spend a lot of time praising God for His amazing goodness to me, but He does not love me more than anybody else. He wants each person to experience His blessings and to be able to respond with a full and grateful heart. He wants each of us to reach stage seven, where we rejoice at the wonders He accomplishes through us.

It Is About Jesus

Have I in some sense "arrived"? If Jesus is the way and if His riches are past finding out, as Paul asserts, then of course I have not arrived. But if "arrived" means that I am going to lock hands with Him and walk under His kingship every day, then I have arrived. I rejoice over what has been. I am excited about what is yet to come.

"If this Flynn is such hot stuff, how come we have never heard of him?" someone might ask. I am not at all hot stuff. I am an average fellow with average natural capabilities. I have never wanted to do more than faithfully pastor whatever church the Lord wanted. By some criteria, they were not spectacular churches. By other criteria, they were amazing places, for the life of Christ grew in them and they obediently did His work. Then in 1994 the Lord fired me during my prayer time and told me to do conferences full-time. So that is what I do. But I refuse to promote Mike Flynn. Who needs *him?* I regularly pray that no one would hear my name unless the Lord has plans for me and my teams to affect them. Because I am so ordinary, the Lord can touch and challenge many to say, "Gee, if God can work through a clod like him, maybe He can use me, too."

It is about Jesus. He is what the world needs to see. But it is also about us when we are confronted with His question: What good am I if I am not good in you? The question is not: "What good am I?" The question is not: "What good are you?" The question focuses on the *combination* of Him and us. "Christ in you, the hope of glory" is how Paul said it (Colossians 1:27). The glory is not Christ, and it is not you—it is *Christ in you.* Now He is plenty glorious on His own. But Paul's point is that the *combination* of you two is what He is after.

Your goodness is born of relationship with Him, submission to His orders, attention to His wishes and display of His qualities. So He can say to you, *Your goodness proves Mine.* He might go on:

> You are the proof of who I say I am. You are the one who shows your world that I am loving. It is you who proves that I am worth believing in. You are the one who demonstrates that I died so people can be forgiven. You are to stay on the alert, watching for the dangers about which I have informed you. You are to be a living example of how large My heart is by giving abundantly of your time, skill, energy and money. You are to manifest My qualities by growing up into the fullness of the stature of Myself. You are to listen for My still, small voice and take action on what I tell you, showing the world that I am a capable, loving, effective Lord.

The Condition of the Heart

What is the condition of our hearts? Though we are extraordinarily blessed by knowing and obeying Jesus, *our* benefit cannot be our primary concern. If it were, we would not be losing our lives. When we exist for the benefit of others, then our hearts are usable and blessable by the One who is the Man for others.

As I mentioned in chapter 4, I learned, for example, that God could not give to me until I adopted a posture of giving to others. When I open my hand to bless others, my hand is open and God can put more into it. But it is not a case of give-to-get, for that would be self-centered. Rather, it is give-to-get-to-give. When your last word is give, your heart is in the right shape.

Containing and giving forth Jesus means that we surrender even our self-originated intentions to help the world. It is not *my* idea of what they need that is important; it is *His* idea of what they need. When we make this surrender, we can relax and let Jesus-in-us express His confident care for others through us. He is the originator, the caregiver, the relaxed and trusting carrier of His life to them.

Our confidence is not in our ability to be used by Him but in His ability to use us. By this confidence we experience peace, we walk in the boldness that He will act, we go forth resting rather than fretting, we stand in other-centeredness.

But this is getting rather otherworldly. Let's get back down to planet Earth. What about the practicalities of surrender?

Surrender

Surrender is a subject that bothers us, and the idea of absolute surrender bothers us absolutely. It looks so much more like death than life. C. S. Lewis said: "The terrible thing, the almost impossible thing, is to hand over your whole self . . . to Christ. But it is far easier than what we are all trying to do instead. For what we are trying to do is remain what we call 'ourselves,' to keep personal happiness as our great aim in life, and yet at the same time to do 'good.' We are all trying to let our minds and hearts go their own way . . . and hoping, in spite of this, to behave honestly and chastely and humbly. And that is exactly what Christ warned us you could not do. A thistle cannot produce figs."[7]

We whine, "This is so *hard,* Lord." To which He replies, *Duh.* Difficulty is not a disqualifier but a goal setter. The problem is that you cannot have both Jesus and you on the throne of your life.

Lewis also stated, "Christ says, 'Give Me all. I don't want so much of your time and so much of your money and so much of your work: I want you. I have not come to torment your natural self, but to kill it. No half-measures are any good. I don't want to cut off a branch here and a branch there, I want to have the whole tree down. . . . Hand over the whole natural self, all the desires which you think innocent as well as the ones you think wicked—the whole outfit. I will give you a new self instead. In fact, I will give you Myself; My own will shall become yours."[8]

Jesus does not want more of you let loose in the world; He wants more of Himself let loose in the world. And He is an incarnator up to His eyebrows. He insists on loosing Himself onto the world *in* you. This means transformation. As someone said, "God is in the business of transformation, not the establishment of a worldwide religious organization."

But transformation is a gradual thing.

So is surrender.

My Experience with Surrender

Most of us cannot truly surrender ourselves absolutely into Jesus' hands because we do not have enough knowledge of ourselves or enough control of ourselves to put everything into His care.

All I can honestly do is state a general intention to surrender to Him and then deal with particular items as they come across the counter. It is in those particular challenges that the proof of the pudding lies.

Part of our faith must be that God minutely oversees the challenges He allows the Spirit or the world to present to us. When the Lord fired me as a pastor and told me to do conferences full-time, it was a bit scary. I knew how to do conferences, but I knew nothing about running what is called a "faith ministry." The whole thing was daunting. But the Lord divided the challenge into smaller pieces, and we just met them as they came up. One decision to make was where to live. Sue and I went on a five-thousand-mile drive to look at communities where we might like to live and base the ministry. It was fascinating how the Lord directed us. In one case, a strong thunderstorm sort of whooshed us through a town in which we were interested. We were not able even to get out of the car. Sue and I looked at each other and said, "I think we're supposed to keep going," which we did.

When we got to Denver, it became apparent that the Lord wanted us to link up with Christ Church, mentioned earlier. Over the next several months the Lord confirmed this decision again and again. It was just one "surrenderable" detail after another. In four days He bought us a house we loved. He recruited a gang of friends to load the moving truck. He brought in the funds we needed to live and work. He informed people of our ministry who booked us to do events. He blessed those events. When our time in Denver was over, He told us to move back to California. He bought us another house we love. He hooked us up with a wonderful church and even put me on the pastoral staff in a part-time role. He recruits self-giving team members—two thousand so far—who pay their way to go on trips to bless other people.

The overall plan is His. The details are ours to agree with and take action on. It is all about surrendering step-by-step. It works. And it is fun.

You

Through this book, these have been my goals for you, dear reader:

- To be taught and motivated to act
- To obey
- To take away some sense of the order of Jesus' commands
- To accept responsibility for displaying Him well
- To lay hold of the understandings and promises that will enable you to obey
- To enjoy the graces available to you
- To lose and, therefore, to gain your life
- To testify by virtue of fullness
- To report for orders daily
- To enjoy present rewards and expect future ones
- To see life and reality through His eyes and, therefore, see them correctly and effectively
- To be encouraged every time you love or believe or forgive or watch or give or grow or listen

Only you can determine if these or better goals have been met. But I am deeply honored to have had your attention for the time it has taken to read this book.

I would like to leave you with a little poem that I hope will be a simple reminder of the seven commands of Jesus:

Love is first, for it's God's own heart;
Believe is next to free His part;
Forgive comes now to honor His blood;
Watch out next so you won't be snubbed;
Give and it will be yours to bless;
Grow up into Christ's fullness;

Hear His whispers to guide your days.
These seven acts will win His praise.

God Has Plans for You

Please give me one more moment. Do not assume that it was a mistake for *you* to have picked up this book. God intended it for you personally. God has great plans for you, and this book is meant to free up some of the understandings, attitudes and behaviors that are needed for you to collaborate more effectively with His plan. He knows and loves you—you personally, you uniquely. You do not have to become anything other than who you are right now for Him to begin taking you to the next stage of benefit and blessing. I urge you to sign up. I urge you to say to Him: "Okay, God, let's go! I trust You to make my life richer and richer. Please tell me what You want me to do next!"

May I pray for you?

Living Lord Jesus, I thank You for this reader. I thank You for the truths and qualities You have deposited in this person's life over many years.

Bless You, Jesus, for having brought this person to the point of faith in Your sacrifice and resurrection.

I thank You for his or her faithfulness to You. Glories to You, Lord, for every victory this person has experienced in forgiveness, health, provision and well-being.

I thank You, Lord, for this person's honesty with You, because I know that You can work with honesty for maximum benefit in his or her relationship with You and others.

Thank You for the goodness You have poured through this person to the world and for the unique revelation of You that this person provides for the world.

And, Lord, I cherish the wonderful plans You have for this reader—the challenges that will bring new victories; the provision that will bring new confidence; the problems whose solutions will bring new encouragement; the wonders of intimacy with You that will bring new excitement and satisfaction.

You are a glorious Lord, and I praise You with all my heart. In the name of Jesus I pray. Amen.

Appendix A

Discipleship Group Discussions

Following is a suggested format for discipleship groups to use this book as a point of discussion. I would suggest that you gather together with the intent of spending about an hour each session. Your group should probably consist of not more than ten or twelve members. Each session, let a member of the group take ten minutes to summarize the chapter being discussed. Then go through the exercises suggested in the following outline.

Chapter 1: The Commands of Christ

1. Share your reactions to Mike's assertion that "we are the Gospel."
2. On a scale of 0 to 10 (poor to excellent), rate how you are doing in showing your world what Christ is like.
3. Discuss Mike's claim that faith must show itself in obedience.
4. Pray for each other for a few minutes.

Chapter 2: The Seventh Command: Hear—*Learn to Hear Like Me*

1. Share your experiences in trying to hear God.

2. Mike spoke of hearing God in Scripture, nature, the supernatural, circumstances, others, peace and surprise thinking. Which of these works best for you? Can you give an example?
3. On what major issue in your life would you like to hear God?
4. Pray for each other to hear God.

Chapter 3: The Sixth Command: Grow Up—*My Goodness Shows as You Grow Up in Me*

1. Mike listed a bunch of Jesus' commands about growing up. Share one or two of those in which you have seen improvement in yourself.
2. Discuss the idea that Jesus wants to look like you and sound like you.
3. In same-gender pairs, go off for thirty minutes and tell your partner something you have never told anyone else about an area with which you struggle. Let your partner pray for you. Then listen to your partner share and pray for him/her.
4. Back in the group, share what it felt like to share and be prayed for. Share what it felt like to listen to your partner and pray for him/her.

Chapter 4: The Fifth Command: Give—*When I Give through You My Goodness Spreads*

1. Share with the group something that is hard for you to give—for example, time, energy or money.
2. If the checkbook is an indicator of where one's heart is, where is your heart?
3. Can you identify with the seven steps of collaboration with Jesus that Mike mentioned on pages 82–84?
4. Share a time when you gave something and how God blessed you for it.
5. Sowing and reaping are both negative and positive. Can you share examples of both positive and negative sowing and reaping?

Chapter 5: The Fourth Command: Watch—*I Want to Be Alert in You*

1. Share a time when you were deceived about God. How did the deception get corrected?
2. Among the things Jesus warns us to watch out for, which is the most important to you at this time?
3. If Jesus comes back while you are still alive, what do you imagine He is going to do with you?

Chapter 6: The Third Command: Forgive—*My Goodness Heals as I Forgive through You*

1. In pairs, tell your partner the thing for which it is most difficult to forgive yourself.
2. Who is the person it is most difficult for you to forgive?
3. Back in the group: Does Mike's assertion that forgiveness is an act of the will make sense to you? Why or why not?
4. While alone, take less than five minutes to experience the following exercise. Think of the worst sin you ever committed. Take thirty seconds to run the videotape of memory: How old were you? Where were you? What did you do? Next, for about fifteen seconds realize that Jesus was close at hand, watching you intently but refusing to be disgusted with your act. Then take about sixty seconds to imagine Him approaching you right at the end of your sin and extending His arms to you. See yourself going into His embrace. Realize that He is comforting you, for your sin has injured you. After a while, take fifteen more seconds to see that He draws back a few inches from you and says, "Will you give Me your guilt?" See yourself saying yes to Him. Then take another minute. See that He reaches into your heart and extracts darkness, which represents your guilt. As you watch, He puts that darkness into His heart where it shrinks until it finally disappears. Then imagine that He takes light out of His heart and puts it into yours where the darkness had been. The light is the opposite of the darkness. Where there had been guilt, there now is forgiveness; where there was injury, there is now healing. Let that transaction sink in. Then decide that the memory of that sin will not manipulate you anymore.

Chapter 7: The Second Command: Believe—*Let Me Help Your Belief*

1. Mike claims that willful faith allows intellectual and emotional benefits to occur ("obedience precedes understanding" and "feelings follow faith"). What is your reaction—positive or negative—to this idea?
2. Remembering Mike's O'Hare airport story, can you recall an instance in your life when you would have been in big trouble if God did not help you? What happened?
3. Mike mentioned a number of faith factors: revelation, the Spirit, vital church life, experiments of faith, taking control of our thoughts. Which one means the most to you at this time in your life?
4. In what generation is your church? What does that make you want to do?

Chapter 8: The First Command: Love—*How Good I Am When I Am Loving in You*

1. Put yourself in God's place: Why do you think He made love the top command?
2. Share an experience or a relationship in which you were changed by someone's love.
3. Who is the person in your life that it is most difficult to love? Would you let the group pray with you about that person?
4. Have you experienced loving discipline from God? Would you share with the group what it was like?

Chapter 9: "Your Goodness Proves Mine"

1. Share with the group the most important thing you have gained from this book.
2. Tell the group what being with them has meant to you.
3. Describe the nature of your relationship with Jesus at this point in your life. For example, rate your closeness to Him (0 = distant, 10 = really close).
4. Does surrender to Jesus look positive or negative to you at this time?

Take a look at the words of this ancient hymn. Which line means the most to you?

Be Thou my vision,
O Lord of my heart,
All else be nought to me,
Save that Thou art;
Be Thou my best thought
In the day and the night,
Both waking and sleeping,
Thy presence my light.

Be Thou my wisdom,
Be Thou my true word,
Be Thou ever with me,
And I with Thee, Lord;
Be Thou my great Father,
And I Thy true son;
Be Thou in me dwelling,
And I with Thee one.

Be Thou my breastplate,
My sword for the fight;
Be Thou my whole armour,
Be Thou my true might;
Be Thou my soul's shelter,
Be Thou my strong tower:
Raise Thou me heavenward,
Great Power of my power.

Riches I heed not,
Nor man's empty praise;
Be Thou mine inheritance
Now and always;
Be Thou and Thou only
The first in my heart:
O Sovereign of heaven,
My treasure Thou art.

High King of heaven,
Thou heaven's bright sun,
O grant me its joys
After vict'ry is won;
Great heart of my own heart,
Whatever befall,
Still be Thou my vision,
O Ruler of all.[1]

Appendix B

About the Baptism with the Holy Spirit

I noted in chapter 3 that the baptism with the Holy Spirit is the event by which God gives us Jesus' abilities and character. Following is the scriptural basis and explanation of the baptism with, or empowerment of, the Holy Spirit.

1. The gift of the Holy Spirit is foretold in all four gospels.

- "He will baptize you with the Holy Spirit and with fire" (Matthew 3:11).
- "I baptize you with water, but he will baptize you with the Holy Spirit" (Mark 1:8).
- "He will baptize you with the Holy Spirit and with fire" (Luke 3:16).
- "The man on whom you see the Spirit come down and remain is he who will baptize with the Holy Spirit" (John 1:33).

2. Each gospel has a form of the Great Commission, and each commission has a proclamation component and a power component.

Proclamation Component	Power Component
"Make disciples" (Matthew 28:19)	"All authority..." (Matthew 28:18).
"Go...and preach" (Mark 16:15)	"And these signs..." (Mark 16:17).
"Repentance and forgiveness of sins will be preached" (Luke 24:47	"I am going to send you what...my Father has promised...power" (Luke 24:49)
"If you forgive...sins" (John 20:23).	"Receive the Holy Spirit" (John 20:22).

3. Jesus said He would send the Holy Spirit.

- "I will ask the Father, and he will give you another Counselor" (John 14:15–16).
- "When the Counselor comes, whom I will send to you from the Father" (John 15:26).
- "I will send him to you" (John 16:7).

4. Jesus breathed on the disciples after the resurrection so they could receive the Holy Spirit.

"And with that he breathed on them and said, 'Receive the Holy Spirit'" (John 20:22).

5. Later still, Jesus told them not to go anywhere until they received (more) power. It appears that Jesus' attitude is that it takes God's power to do God's work.

- "But stay in the city until you have been clothed with power from on high" (Luke 24:49).
- "But wait for the gift my Father promised . . . but in a few days you will be baptized with the Holy Spirit. . . . But you will receive power when the Holy Spirit comes on you" (Acts 1:4–5, 8).

6. The promise of Jesus and Joel 2:28 is fulfilled on the Day of Pentecost.

- Acts 2 tells of tongues, prophecy and empowered preaching.
- In Acts 2:41, previously frightened Peter is now used to boldly save three thousand people.

7. The rest of Acts tells of power breaking out.

8. The Gentiles experience Pentecost.

- "The Holy Spirit came on all who heard the message" (Acts 10:44).

9. Apparently all believers are meant to receive this baptism with the Holy Spirit.

- Philip in Samaria (Acts 8:14–17)
- Paul in Ephesus (Acts 19:1–7)

10. Varieties of gifts (Jesus' abilities) are available in the power of the Holy Spirit.

- 1 Corinthians 12:7 *phaneroosis* = manifestations
- 1 Corinthians 14:12 *pneumatoon* = spirituals
- Romans 12:6 *charismata* = gifts or gracelets
- Ephesians 4:7 *doreas* = person-gifts or gifted persons

11. The fruit of the Spirit can be experienced (Jesus' character qualities).

- "But the fruit of the Spirit is love, joy, peace, patience, kindness, goodness, faithfulness, gentleness and self-control" (Galatians 5:22).

12. Ways in which people are filled with the Holy Spirit vary.

- *at the same moment* as conversion (Acts 19:5)
- *after* having received Jesus as Savior (Acts 8.15; 9:17)
- *before* having confessed Jesus as Savior (Acts 10:44)
- *sovereignly* (Acts 2:1–4; 10:44)
- *through the laying on of hands* (Acts 8:15; 9:17; 19:5)

13. A clarification.

- All who have received Jesus as Savior already have the Holy Spirit *in* them. This is for salvation, becoming a child of God, standing to inherit eternal life and for membership in the universal Body of Christ. The appropriate sacrament is baptism.

- The baptism with the Holy Spirit is for empowerment and for fruit bearing. This is being *filled* with the Spirit. The appropriate sacrament in liturgical churches is confirmation, which can also be called the "ordination of the laity."

14. A suggested prayer to receive the baptism with the Holy Spirit.

"Lord Jesus, I now affirm that You are my Savior and that I have professed You as my Savior and Lord. I acknowledge that You are the only way to the Father and that You have entered my heart, given me new birth and pledge to forgive my sins every time I confess them.

"What is more, You are also the Baptizer with the Holy Spirit. In preparation for asking You to fill me with the Holy Spirit:

- I confess my sins and ask You to forgive me.
- I repent of and renounce any involvement in spiritual forces that are not of You (astrology, transcendental meditation, shakras, palm reading, divination, tarot cards, occult religions/ practices, New Age spirituality, auras, healing by means other than those sanctioned by Scripture, etc.).

"I wish to be empowered by the Holy Spirit for fruitfulness and giftedness in relationship with and service to You.

"Therefore, Lord Jesus, I ask You to fill me with the Holy Spirit. And by faith—as exercised by my will—I declare that You are filling me with the Holy Spirit, whether or not I feel anything. And I thank You."

15. We are assured that if we ask for it, we will receive it.

- "Which of you fathers, if your son asks for a fish, will give him a snake instead? Or if he asks for an egg, will give him a scorpion? If you then, though you are evil, know how to give good gifts to your children, *how much more will your Father in heaven give the Holy Spirit to those who ask him!*" (Luke 11:11–13).
- "But wait for the gift my Father promised, which you have heard me speak about. For John baptized with water, but in a few days you *will* be baptized with the Holy Spirit" (Acts 1:4–5).

- "But you *will* receive power when the Holy Spirit comes on you; and you will be my witnesses in Jerusalem, and in all Judea and Samaria, and to the ends of the earth" (Acts 1:8).
- "*All* of them were filled with the Holy Spirit and began to speak in other tongues as the Spirit enabled them" (Acts 2:4).

16. Functions of the Spirit.

   A. Gifts (Romans 12; 1 Corinthians 12–14; Ephesians 4)
   B. Fruit (Galatians 5:22)
   C. And much more:
      1. Romans

2:29	circumcises the heart
5:5	sheds abroad the love of the Father in our hearts
8:4	enables us to live
8:9	should control us
8:14	leads us
8:26	helps us in our weakness
8:27	intercedes for the saints (through our groans)
14:17	gives us righteousness, peace and joy
15:13	overflows us with hope
15:16	sanctifies us
15:19	by His power, performs signs and miracles

      2. 1 Corinthians

2:10	searches all things
2:12	enables us to understand what God has given us
2:13	teaches us
3:16	lives in us as His temple
6:11	justifies us in the name of the Lord Jesus
12:3	enables us to say, "Jesus is Lord"
12:4	gives different gifts to the Body
12:7	manifests Himself in believers

      3. 2 Corinthians

1:22	has been put in our hearts by the Father as a deposit
3:6	enables us to be ministers of a new covenant
3:17	gives freedom
3:18	gives ever-increasing glory
13:14	fellowships with us all

4. Galatians
   - 3:2   comes in response to hearing with faith
   - 3:5   enables us to work miracles by faith
   - 3:14   gives us the promise of the Spirit through faith
   - 4:6   enables us to cry out, "Abba!"
   - 5:22   makes us fruitful
   - 6:8   gives us eternal life

5. Ephesians
   - 1:13   is a seal
   - 1:17   gives wisdom and revelation
   - 2:18   gives us access to the Father
   - 3:5   reveals matters to us
   - 3:16   impacts our inner being
   - 4:3   enables us to keep unity and peace
   - 4:30   can be grieved
   - 5:18   fills us
   - 6:18   enables us to pray on all occasions

6. Notice: These are not new things to you. The Holy Spirit has been at work in your life for a very long time!

17. Things the Spirit does.

A. Convicts (not condemns)

"When the people heard this, they were cut to the heart" (Acts 2:37).

B. Heals

"Does God give you his Spirit and work miracles among you because you observe the law, or because you believe what you heard?" (Galatians 3:5).

C. Blesses

"Joy given by the Holy Spirit" (1 Thessalonians 1:6).

D. Comforts

"And encouraged by the Holy Spirit, [the church] grew in numbers" (Acts 9:31).

E. Anoints

"Do not neglect your gift, which was given you through a prophetic message when the body of elders laid their hands on you" (1 Timothy 4:14).

F. Directs
   "Set apart for me Barnabas and Saul for the work to which I have called them" (Acts 13:2).
G. The Holy Spirit works in agreement with Scripture but is not limited to it. The Bible is the menu, not the meal; it points to the kinds of things we can do with the direction, empowerment and collaboration of God. With the Spirit, we can be doers of a living Word and not merely hearers of the Word.

18. Ways to relate with the Holy Spirit.

A. Talk to Him.
   - "Good morning, Holy Spirit, thank You for this new day. Thank You that You are going to help me live for Jesus today."
   - "Well, Holy Spirit, we are going to speak to this guy down the hall about the Lord Jesus. Give me Your words for him, Lord."
B. Listen to Him.
   - Learn to dial down and relax, so He can get information from your spirit into your mind.
C. Discern Him.
   - Learn to sense His peace or agitation in your heart, passing judgment on ideas, intentions and plans that are in line with Scripture.
D. Obey Him. He is *God*.
E. Trust Him
F. Praise Him.
   - "All right, Holy Spirit! Way to go! Thank You for healing that person!"
   - "I love You, Holy Spirit. And I love what You did for that person."

Appendix C

The Two Trees in the Garden

I now want to share with you a comparison of two trees in early Genesis. I first ran into this comparison through a section in Ted Haggard's *Primary Purpose.* Later I found a sermon by Ted on the subject. I am indebted to him for providing a window into attitudinal realities that have set me and kept me free. Many of the following thoughts are his.[1]

I have printed the comparison of these two trees in the sermon notes form I use when preaching it. These notes zero in on a choice we have to make concerning the attitudes we bear toward life. Most of the notes are printed in either a left- or right-hand format in order to emphasize visually which attitude we are dealing with. Read each page top to bottom. The connection with this chapter will become apparent as we are exhorted to watch out for judgment.

In the middle of the garden were the tree of life and the tree of the knowledge of good and evil (Genesis 2:9).

And the LORD God commanded the man, "You are free to eat from any tree in the garden; but you must not eat from the tree of the knowledge of good and evil, for when you eat of it you will surely die" (Genesis 2:16).

The comparison of these two trees is about how to live the life of Jesus. The two trees stood for obedience and disobedience.

Every day we have a choice to live in the Tree of Life or the Tree of the Knowledge of Good and Evil. When we eat of the Tree of the Knowledge of Good and Evil, we enter into our own value system. The Tree of Life is walking in the life—the value system—that the Lord Jesus has to offer each one of us.

Before the Fall, there were God and Adam and Eve. They had fellowship, experienced mutual enjoyment, were able to laugh easily, to dance and to grin. The Tree of Life is a picture of walking the Spirit-filled life—no grudges, no heartache, no bitterness.

Things happen that can cause bitterness, but if we choose to live in the Tree of Life, we can turn the other cheek. If we live in the Tree of the Knowledge of Good and Evil, however, we draw back and blast those who offend us. We know and articulate what they did wrong, and we know that we are God's instruments to make them right. So we jam our fists down their throats.

So the Tree of Life and the Tree of the Knowledge of Good and Evil are decisions that we get to make every day.

Let's spend a few minutes contrasting these two trees.

Tree of Life	Tree of the Knowledge of Good and Evil
	A formulation of a value system about what is good and what is evil.
	What is good in me? What is evil in me?
	What is good in you? What is evil in you?
	Whom do I dislike because they are evil?
	Whom do I have to destroy because they are evil? Whom do I need to embrace because they have done good things? All those things bring us death.
	If you become an expert in what is good, you will die.
	You will judge yourself and others so that you will die.
	If you become an expert in what is evil, the result is the same.
But being an expert in maintaining life—forgiving and refusing to judge—promotes the life and freedom and flow of God.	
	If you choose good you die.
	If you choose evil you die.
	If you choose death you die.
	If you choose the Tree of the Knowledge of Good and Evil, you experience death, whether you are a religious or an unreligious person.

Tree of Life	Tree of the Knowledge of Good and Evil
If you choose life you live. This lets you walk in freedom—free of guilt, anger, bitterness, judgment and heartache.	
	There are those who are experts in the Scriptures, but they are dead. They are saved but unable to flow in the life of God. This is learning the Bible from the Tree of the Knowledge of Good and Evil perspective.
Reading the Bible from the Tree of Life perspective, however, makes the Bible a life-giving implement.	
	If you are hurt, offended or bitter, then you have gotten into the Tree of the Knowledge of Good and Evil. This tree is marked by legalism, exclusive revelation and an attitude that everyone else is wrong. This makes the Bible a weapon of tyranny.
Instead, let the Scriptures minister life to you. The woman taken in adultery was ministered to in this way; she was forgiven, set free and restored by Jesus.	
	The Pharisees wanted her to stop her adultery, too, but they approached her from a Tree of the Knowledge of Good and Evil perspective. You can know you are right but be internally all wrong. Those who are offended become experts on who is right and wrong. We do not need to be experts on right and wrong or good and evil; we need to realize how to get the life of God into people's hearts. When Adam and Eve took from the Tree of the Knowledge of Good and Evil, their eyes were opened and they could now experience shame, legalism, inadequacy and covering up. This knowledge is all around us in our world today; almost every headline we read has something to do with a cover-up.

To Sum Up Briefly

Those who have a Tree of Life perspective:	Those who have a Tree of the Knowledge of Good and Evil perspective:
—Go to church to grow in the love of God.	—Go to church to keep up an attendance record.
—Read the Bible to discover the love, mercy and life of God. This is freeing, joyful and promotes life.	—Read the Bible to count up brownie points with God and man. This is harsh, critical and promotes death.
—Might say: "Thanks for coming to church today. It blesses me to see you and hear you worship God."	—Might say: "Where were you last week? Don't you know that you can't please God unless you attend church every week?"

Tree of Life	Tree of the Knowledge of Good and Evil
—Are open to God. God is their best friend. And in the Tree of Life they are able to keep no record of wrongs, to release others in forgiveness and to trust God to be their defender. God is more concerned with your heart's condition than if you are right.	—Are closed to God and are hiding from Him. Are characterized by fear and shame. Are aware of nakedness. Blame others and displace responsibility. But being right is irrelevant because it does not open the Kingdom. Rather, it closes the Kingdom to others. One could say they are "dead right."
—Let God handle judgment.	—Try to handle judgment themselves, but their hearts cannot handle judgment.
—Keep God as their Lord. They forgive others, keeping them from being lord, from consuming their thoughts and from becoming bitter. If someone slaps their cheek, they give them the other cheek, then walk a mile with them and then pray with them. That drives demons crazy. And it drives crazy those people who want to manipulate us into hating them. It keeps them from gaining control in our lives. It allows us to maintain innocence.	
	—Make the person they are blaming their lord. This is what happens when you displace responsibility. "Eve made me do it" is the same thing as saying "Eve is my lord." A victim points out the perpetrator of his or her victimization and makes the perpetrator lord. So Eve was Adam's lord, and the snake was Eve's lord. That is what unforgiveness always does. The one you do not forgive is your lord. "I can't do it right because they made a mistake; they screwed up. They offended me. They ruined my life." This is totally giving your life over to those who have wronged you.
	—Try to get everyone on their team. They want to tell you who to hate and why. "We're good; they're bad. We're right; they're wrong." They try to get others to take on their offense, which effectively takes them out of the role of peacekeepers and reconcilers.
—Know that there is only one enemy, and he is the devil. No human being on earth is your enemy. If you think a human is your enemy, love him, pray for him and bless him—that is what Jesus said to do to human enemies. This keeps them from getting their claws into you and it helps them get out of the Tree of the Knowledge of Good and Evil.

Jesus modeled this simple, beautiful innocence for us, and He had the most vicious enemies of all. With innocence comes the anointing. | |

Tree of Life	Tree of the Knowledge of Good and Evil
	Blaming others leads to victimization. There is no anointing in being a victim. All a victim can do is say, "I'm all beat up. I can't make it. They've stolen my life from me." For example, the cause of African Americans in our country was set back after the death of Martin Luther King when some of their leaders fell into being victims. When blacks started telling themselves they were victims of white people, they empowered white people to run their lives. White people should not be their lord; Jesus should be their Lord. Similarly, it is time women stopped making men their lords. I thank God we are coming to a period in this country's life when no ethnic group will be a majority. Only Jesus can be anyone's Lord. Whatever Jesus calls you to be, you can be so long as you don't fall into victimization. Moishe Rosen says of his Jewish culture: "What a burden upon one's soul to feel obligated to despise others! How that 'duty' of remembering the wrong done to one's people can keep a person from happiness! That kind of grudge is a cancer that eats out the vitality of the spirit. It creates perpetual alienation from all except those who share the same morbid grudge. Thus, my people have become a fellowship of the wronged, an association of the persecuted, the perpetual victims of their neighbors. Our noble religion, revealed by God, is perverted to become the reason for our defensiveness."[2]
George Washington Carver said, "I will never let another man ruin my life by making me hate him." He was an African-American man who stayed in innocence during a terrible time in American history. He would go into the forest each evening and kneel and forgive the people who were treating him so badly. Because of that he was able to be a tremendous innovator and thinker.	

Let's Sum Up Again

Freedom, joy, innocence	Captivity, guilt, self-righteousness
Jesus is the Head of the Church	Whoever is right is head of the Church
Jesus seeks the broken, the lost, the guilty so that He can rescue them	Hide from Jesus in brokenness, lostness and guilt
Ability to straightforwardly admit guilt and receive forgiveness	Blame others. "It is someone else's fault."
Though confused, they know they can trust Jesus	When confused, they look for someone who can be held accountable

Tree of Life	Tree of the Knowledge of Good and Evil
Jesus is Lord	Blame others, which leads to victimization, which leads to the loss of the Lordship of Jesus

In choosing the Tree of Life we have life-giving innocence. We gain a clear-eyed look of acknowledging our troubles, but we place them and ourselves under the Saviorhood and Lordship of Jesus. For example, we lost a pregnancy—three of them in fact—but we got healed and moved on, and the memory of them does not restrict us. Innocence is not ignorance, not naiveté, not a lack of critical thinking, not a poor education. Innocence is a determination to respond to this terrible world in a godly fashion.

Everybody gets offended; everybody has somebody do bad things to him or her. What makes the difference is how we respond to them. People can horribly violate us and we can have nothing in our hearts against them. We can take action toward others from the Tree of Life but not from the Tree of the Knowledge of Good and Evil.

The natural consequence of walking in the Tree of Life is a free flow of the Spirit: the gifts and the fruit. I have seen the ministry of the Spirit flow in someone who does not fully understand redemption because they were in the Tree of Life, and I have seen experts in the Bible who were perched in the Tree of the Knowledge of Good and Evil who could not move in the Holy Spirit at all. Our thinking determines how we are. Think in life or think in knowledge is the choice.

"In him was life, and that life was the light of men" (John 1:4).

"I am the bread of life" (John 6:35, 48).

"I am the living bread" (John 6:51).

"[I am] living water" (John 4:10).

Walking with Him is the substance, the food, of godly life. Being good is not our goal; being godly is.

Jesus is wrapped up in life. His purpose is life. We do not go to heaven because we are good but because we know life Himself.

"Now if we died with Christ, we believe that we will also live with him. . . . Count yourselves . . . alive to God in Christ Jesus" (Romans 6:8–11).

Final Summary	
Rescue people	Judge people
Refuse to be victims of anyone	Be victimized and complain
Let Jesus set the agenda for ministry	Let those we criticize set the agenda

Tree of Life	Tree of the Knowledge of Good and Evil
Maintain our innocence	Lose our innocence
Maintain healthy attitudes	Succumb to toxic attitudes
Live!	Die!
Be forgiving	Be right
Take responsibility	Turn over responsibility to others
Intercede	Manipulate
Act	React

Finally, if you criticize someone for being in the Tree of the Knowledge of Good and Evil, which tree are *you* in? The only way to get someone out of the Tree of the Knowledge of Good and Evil is from the Tree of Life.

Notes

Chapter 1: The Commands of Christ

1. Kelly Smith, "What Good Is Jesus?" (Arvada, Colo.: Mama Rose Music, 2000).

2. George MacDonald and Michael Phillips, eds., *Knowing the Heart of God* (Minneapolis, Minn.: Bethany House Publishers, 1990), 30f.

3. Mike Flynn, *The Mustard Seed Book* (Grand Rapids, Mich.: Chosen Books, 1995). Reprinted by FreshWind Ministries, 2001. Available through FreshWind Ministries, 811 Moby Dick Lane, Oxnard, CA 93030.

4. Ruth Ruibal, *Unity in the Spirit* (Lynwood, Wash.: TransformNations Media, 2002), 110.

5. C. S. Lewis, *Mere Christianity* (San Francisco: HarperSanFrancisco, 2001), 195.

6. W. H. Lewis, ed., *Letters of C. S. Lewis* (New York: Harcourt Brace Jovanovich, 1996), 210–11.

Chapter 2: The Seventh Command: Hear

1. I am indebted to my mentor, John Wimber, for my initial learning of these factors.

Chapter 3: The Sixth Command: Grow Up

1. Mike Flynn, *Holy Vulnerability* (Grand Rapids, Mich.: Chosen Books, 1990), 147f.

2. John Wimber, *Kingdom Living* (Ann Arbor, Mich.: Servant Publications), 9.

3. Norman P. Grubb, *Who Am I?* (Fort Washington, Pa.: Christian Literature Crusade, 1978), 59.

Chapter 4: The Fifth Command: Give

1. Contact me at mkfln@aol.com or at FreshWind Ministries, 811 Moby Dick Lane, Oxnard, CA 93030, and I will send you directions on how to take in strangers safely.

2. Mike Flynn, *Making Disciples* (Oxnard, Calif.: FreshWind Ministries, 1997), 4.

Chapter 5: The Fourth Command: Watch

1. Ruibal, *Unity in the Spirit*, 111.

2. Flynn, *The Mustard Seed Book*.

3. MacDonald, *Knowing the Heart of God*, 5.

4. Six parables have exclusivity as their focus: the barren fig tree, rich fool, unmerciful servant, unworthy servants, fig tree and wicked tenants. Nine parables have the main point of inclusivity: the friend at midnight, workers in the vineyard, lost coin, lost son, two debtors, persistent widow, shrewd manager, wise servant and lost sheep. Eighteen have either inclusivity or exclusivity as the point: the net, Good Samaritan, great banquet, householder, wedding banquet, Pharisee and tax collector, ten minas, rich man and Lazarus, sheep and goats, weeds, talents, ten virgins, two sons, wedding feast, house on the rock, new cloth, new wine in old wineskins and the parable of the sower.

Chapter 6: The Third Command: Forgive

1. Alan Paton, "Meditation for a Young Boy Confirmed," Stanza XIII (Cincinnati: Forward Movement Publications, 1954, reprinted 1985).

2. C. S. Lewis, *The Great Divorce* (New York: Macmillan, 1946), 72.

3. In other books I have dealt with the intention-behavior glitch: *Holy Vulnerability*, 50; *Inner Healing* by Mike Flynn and Doug Gregg (Downers Grove, Ill.: InterVarsity Press, 1993), 136.

4. *The Mustard Seed Book* deals with this in depth.

5. George MacDonald, *Unspoken Sermons*, series one (Eureka, Calif.: J. Joseph Flynn Rare Books in association with Sunrise Books, 1989), 74–76.

6. Walter B. Knight, *Knight's Illustrations for Today* (Chicago: Moody Press, 1970), 122.

Chapter 7: The Second Command: Believe

1. Flynn, *Holy Vulnerability*, 23–26.

2. Watchman Nee, *The Spiritual Man*, vol. III (New York: Christian Fellowship Publishers, 1968), 93.

3. Ibid.

4. A 60-page Healing Course syllabus with tapes contains this teaching and can be ordered from FreshWind Ministries, 811 Moby Dick Lane, Oxnard, CA 93030 or mkfln@aol.com.

5. V. Raymond Edman, *They Found the Secret* (Grand Rapids, Mich.: Zondervan, 1960, 1984), 20.

Chapter 8: The First Command: Love

1. This mode of ministry is dealt with in some depth in *Inner Healing*, 200–203.

2. This quote comes from a newsletter article I read thirty years ago. The article is called "Key Words Which Unlock Scripture," and the author is Duane Edward Spencer.

3. Tim Cullen, "Hallelujah, My Father" (Millport, Isle of Cumbrae, Scotland: Celebration Services Ltd., 1975).

4. Letters of C. S. Lewis (undated), para. 1, p. 231, published in *The Quotable Lewis*, eds. W. Martindale and J. Root (Wheaton, Ill.: Tyndale House Publishers, Inc., 1989), 408.

5. MacDonald, *Unspoken Sermons*, 74–76.

6. Gary Smalley, "Love Is a Decision" video series (Grand Rapids, Mich.: Zondervan Films).

7. The prose is titled "Love," by Emmet Fox, 1886–1951.

8. MacDonald, *Unspoken Sermons*, 74–76.

Chapter 9: "Your Goodness Proves Mine"

1. George MacDonald, *Unspoken Sermons*, series two (Eureka, Calif.: J. Joseph Flynn Rare Books in association with Sunrise Books, 1989), 244–45.

2. Edman, *They Found the Secret*, 21.

3. Ibid., 170.

4. MacDonald, *Unspoken Sermons*, series two, 124, 126.

5. Grubb, 59.

6. MacDonald, *Unspoken Sermons*, various.

7. Lewis, *Mere Christianity*, 197–98.

8. Ibid.

Appendix A

1. Mary Elizabeth Byrne (trans: Eleanor Henrietta Hull), *Be Thou My Vision*.

Appendix C

1. Ted Haggard, "The Tree of Life" (Colorado Springs, Colo.: New Life Church, 11/27/1994). This teaching is available on tape by calling 719-594-6602.

2. *The Jews for Jesus Newsletter*, vol. 6:5746 (1986).

The **Reverend Mike Flynn,** an Episcopal priest and Vineyard pastor, is director of FreshWind Ministries. FreshWind's vision is "teaching, modeling and imparting responsiveness to the Holy Spirit for life and ministry."

FreshWind has sponsored more than 375 conferences in the United States and overseas to which more than 2,100 team members have traveled, at their own expense, to minister to participants. Subject areas include: "The Words and Works of Jesus"; "Healing—Physical, Emotional, Spiritual and Relational"; "Leadership Development"; "Lay Ministry Development"; "Congregational Development"; "Spiritual Growth"; "Ministry to the Poor"; "Intimacy with God"; "Catch the Wind"; "Growing in Prayer" and "Learning to Use Effective Faith."

FreshWind has been engaged by Episcopalians, Vineyards, Methodists, Presbyterians, Adventists, Anglicans and Foursquare, as well as by the Order of St. Luke, seminaries, Bible schools, missions agencies and independent churches and organizations.

Mike has written several other books that elicit heartfelt responses from their readers. These can be ordered from the contacts below or from Amazon.com:

Holy Vulnerability: The Risks and Rewards of Opening Up to God
Inner Healing: A Handbook for Helping Yourself and Others (with Doug Gregg)
The Mustard Seed Book: Understanding and Using Effective Faith
Making Disciples: Following Jesus' Model

For more information about the ministry of Mike and FreshWind, or to explore the possibility of an event, contact:

The Rev. Mike Flynn, Director
FreshWind Ministries
811 Moby Dick Lane
Oxnard, CA 93030
(805) 487-9259
mkfln@aol.com
www.freshwindministries.org